A CRASH COURSE

PSYCHOLOGY

A CRASH COURSE

PSYCHOLOGY

PAUL CARSLAKE & RAZWANA QUADIR

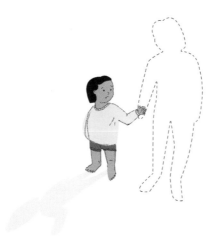

IVY PRESS

First published in the UK in 2019 by
Ivy Press
An imprint of The Quarto Group
The Old Brewery, 6 Blundell Street
London N7 9BH, United Kingdom
T (0)20 7700 6700 **F** (0)20 7700 8066
www.QuartoKnows.com

British Library Cataloguing-in-Publication Data
A catalogue record for this book is available
from the British Library

ISBN: 978-1-78240-869-7

This book was conceived, designed, and produced by
Ivy Press
58 West Street, Brighton BN1 2RA, United Kingdom

Publisher Susan Kelly
Editorial Director Tom Kitch
Art Director James Lawrence
Project Editor Stephanie Evans
Copy Editor Angela Koo
Design JC Lanaway
Illustrator Elise Gaignet
Design Manager Anna Stevens
Series Concept Design Michael Whitehead

Printed in China

10 9 8 7 6 5 4 3 2 1

INTRODUCTION   6

SCHOOLS OF THOUGHT   10

TIMELINE   18

1 **DEVELOPMENT & LANGUAGE**   **20**

2 **PERCEPTION & COGNITION**   **52**

3 **SOCIAL PSYCHOLOGY**   **84**

4 **PSYCHOLOGY OF DIFFERENCE**   **116**

GLOSSARY   148

FURTHER READING   152

INDEX   156

ABOUT THE AUTHORS   159

ACKNOWLEDGMENTS   160

INTRODUCTION

The fact that you have picked up—and possibly bought—this book suggests you have a certain curiosity about psychology. It could be an interest in why people behave as they do. How we decide—or don't. What we notice and fail to notice. Why good people do bad things. How we make sense of events. Or why we seem to be hardwired to react in a certain way every time: how we think, how we communicate, even how we fall in love. In short, how our minds work and how we manage to live in this world alongside other people.

What is psychology?

Psychology is the science of the mind and behavior. It is a huge field, but a relatively young science. For centuries, questions about the mind and the idea of the individual self were the domain of philosophers (and, in fact, there is a book on that subject in this same series). During the nineteenth century, physicians took an interest in the brain, beginning to realize, for example, through the evidence of patients with head injuries, that certain parts of the brain seemed to control certain behaviors, including what appeared to be emotional responses. But it was only toward the end of the nineteenth century that the science of psychology really got started, first with the "introspectionists" working on consciousness, awareness, and memory in laboratory experiments, followed soon after by decades of psychological

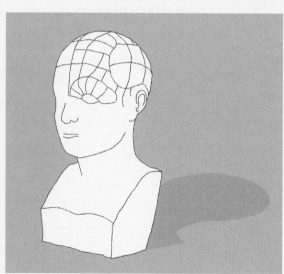

experimentation by the "behaviorists," who were interested in how humans have a propensity to respond to stimulus—to the point where our behavior might be overwhelmingly driven by "conditioning" and "reinforcement." Ivan Pavlov's laboratory dogs are the classic example.

Around the same time, at the turn of the twentieth century, a totally different and competing approach emerged: that of Sigmund Freud and psychoanalysis, with, for the first time, a complete theory about the internal world of our minds—something impossible to test in the lab, but a theory that gained enormous traction for the ensuing

fifty years, particularly in the treatment of certain types of mental illness. By the middle of the twentieth century, a new and important strand of psychology came to the fore, looking at how we make sense of the world around us and the events that we encounter: cognitive psychology. This is a vast field of psychology that brings together every aspect of our outside worlds with the thinking and processing of our minds: a field that is populated not only by experimental psychologists, but also by information-processing experts and neuroscientists.

Psychology has branched out extensively in recent years, covering all aspects of mental life and human behavior, and extending its knowledge and explorations into medicine, neuroscience, computer science, clinical interventions, and self-help, as well as into politics, economics, and the law. Its findings can be applied to us all in some capacity or at some point in our lives, from the everyday decisions we make about what to wear or what to eat, to the bigger questions about who we are and what we believe, and ultimately to our sense of well-being (or not). The importance of mental health has received an increasing spotlight over recent years and poor mental health is no longer seen as something to be ashamed of or hidden away, but something that demands due attention and care. Our mental health is inextricably tied to our physical well-being, and the ability to live healthy, happy, and functioning lives. The importance of understanding human psychology and its effective application in our lives cannot be denied.

Casting off the old clichés

While the discipline itself has evolved, so have its practitioners. If you think of a psychologist, what kind of image do you have in mind? In the many cartoons featuring psychology jokes, we usually see a balding, middle-age man wearing a lab coat. Much of the research in this book comes from a time when the constraints and biases of society during the twentieth century meant that women had few opportunities to study for a Ph.D., let alone to lead a research department. The same was true for most ethnic minorities, with a few notable exceptions. A survey in 2002 of the "100 Most Eminent Psychologists of the Twentieth Century" came up with 95 men and just 5 women.

Today, however, the picture is changing. In 1975, only 30 percent of Ph.D. students in psychology in the US were women. Currently, the figure is more than 70 percent, and around three-quarters of early-career psychologists today are women, a trend that can be seen worldwide.

How the "crash course" works

Finally, a word on how this book is organized. We have grouped the 52 topics into four main chapters, preceded by some explanations of the various schools of thought in psychology that provide a little historical context. Our first main chapter, **Development & Language**, looks at how we learn and develop, both as social beings, and as individuals, learning to think and to communicate and understand the unspoken rules that govern our behavior. Chapter 2 brings together some of the most famous experimenters in the field of **Perception & Cognition**, from studies of memory and perception, through to the ways in which we can deceive ourselves, and the role played in all this by emotion. Our third chapter, **Social Psychology**, provides a glimpse into some fascinating research on the extraordinary ways in which we interact and are influenced by others; and the final chapter, **Psychology of Difference**, looks at the ways in which humans, although similar in form and needs, differ, with a focus on personality and the realms of "abnormality."

It is of course impossible to try to embrace the whole of psychology in this short book, but the point of a crash course is to cover as much ground as possible at high speed, a kind of freeway journey to knowledge. Of course, the trouble with freeways is we can't always appreciate the landscape around us, and it can pay dividends to take the exit ramp and explore the terrain in more detail and at a leisurely pace. We hope this book will at least show you what's out there. After that, we'll leave it to your own curiosity to lead you to further discoveries.

How to use this book

This book distills the current body of knowledge into 52 manageable chunks, so that you can either skim-read or delve in a bit deeper. There are four chapters, each containing 13 topics, prefaced by a set of biographies of key psychologists in the field. The introduction to each chapter gives an overview of some of the main concepts you might need to navigate the topics.

Each topic has three paragraphs.

The Main Concept provides an overview of the theory.

The Wider Picture shows how thinking about the concept has developed or changed direction.

The Evidence provides a short summary of an experiment or set of experiments or studies which support (or in some cases challenge) the main concept.

The four principal schools of thought are set out on pages 10–17, followed by a timeline of the milestones in psychology over more than a century and a quarter.

PSYCHOANALYSIS

Before Sigmund Freud and psychoanalysis, the medical study of the mind in the nineteenth century had become focused on the brain's structure, with the idea that psychiatric illnesses were the result of neural damage to the brain. Freud himself trained as a neurologist, but his investigations into cases of "hysteria" (where patients' physical symptoms had no apparent physiological cause) led him to believe that the roots of the illness lay in past traumatic events that had been buried—repressed—in the unconscious. In numerous cases he noted that, once a patient had remembered and faced up to such an event, their symptoms cleared. This prompted Freud to develop a complete theory of the human mind, the first to be attempted, and one that he continued to refine, adapt, and expand until shortly before his death in 1939.

The conscious and the unconscious

Freud's model included two basic animal drives—pleasure-seeking and aggression—that provide the energy for everything we do. The mind was likened to an iceberg, the tip being the conscious part of it, with the rest of it an unseen, deep, massive unconscious, containing locked-away thoughts and conflicts. Freud believed that the unconscious made itself felt through dreams, or slips of the tongue, or could be interpreted through analysis. Later, he added to his "topographical" model, bringing in a "structural" model, with its three competing drives: the unruly "id," representing uninhibited drives; the judgmental super-ego, acting as an inner voice of conscience and control; and the ego—or self—trying to mediate between this inner world and the reality of the world outside. To function successfully in society, Freud claimed, the energy of these instinctive drives need to be channeled into other meaningful activities, such as work or creativity—a process called "sublimation." For Freud, psychic problems—neuroses, or the more serious psychoses—had their roots in early developmental conflicts, specifically the "Oedipus Complex" where a child realizes it is part of a triangular relationship with its parents, and has to negotiate a set of sexual jealousies, anxieties, and fantasies provoked by this realization.

Freud was not alone in exploring the psychoanalytic approach. In 1912, Carl Jung published *Psychology of the Unconscious*, which diverged from Freud over two key issues. The first was the importance of sexuality. For Jung, sexual drive was just one kind of life force, not the main one. The second was the unconscious, which, for Jung, contained all our memories and thoughts, not just bad ones. Jung also believed that alongside the individual unconscious sat a collective unconscious, a kind of "reservoir" of all human experience. His theories anticipated much later work on personality theory, by setting down markers on introversion and extraversion as well as bringing in a wide-ranging social dimension—far removed from Freud's more self-contained internal world.

After Freud's death, his daughter Anna added to the theoretical base with psychoanalytic work with children. In the UK, other psychoanalytic thinkers rose to prominence, including Melanie Klein with her speculations on the frightening inner terrors experienced by newborn infants, and her theory of how people may "split" themselves from painful or dangerous thoughts and come to see them as residing in others instead. The school of "object relations" took up the idea of the self being built upon "internalized objects"—for example, inner-world representations of real people, a view that led to a set of theories about the mechanisms of depression, mourning, and even self-harm. By the 1950s, some psychoanalytic theorists added a social dimension, including Donald Winnicott, who investigated the powerful psychological connection between infant and mother, around the same time that attachment theory was taking off.

New ways of thinking

Psychoanalysis held sway over clinical psychology throughout the first half of the twentieth century, gradually ceding ground to new behavioral and cognitive therapies. Freud himself took a scientific approach, willing to drop elements of his theory if a better explanation came to light, but many of his later followers were more protective of his ideas than perhaps Freud himself would have been as new thinking emerged. It may be helpful to view Freud as a kind of Isaac Newton figure who started a whole new avenue of thinking. As the analytic theorist Harry Guntrip put it: "It is not the function of the pioneer to say the last word but to say the first word."

BEHAVIORAL PSYCHOLOGY

The discipline of psychology began in earnest in the late nineteenth century (before Freud), with its roots in the study of philosophy. It was led in the United States by William James, while in Germany Wilhelm Wundt and Hermann Ebbinghaus began lab-based experiments that set high scientific standards for the subject. The problem was that, as with philosophy, the early study of psychology centered on thought and the internal workings of the mind—the so-called "introspectionist" approach. One experimenter might find that "when I do this, I experience this," yet another doing the same thing could experience a completely different result.

By the twentieth century, however, advances in the physical sciences led to a change of track toward a psychological science that would also deliver hard evidence observable in the physical world. This new approach became known as behaviorism and was first spelled out in John B. Watson's now-famous 1913 lecture "Psychology as the Behaviorist Views It." The aim, above all, was to make psychology into an experimental branch of natural science.

Only study what can be measured

The foundation of the behavioral approach was that for humans, like any other organism, a stimulus will lead to a response, and this is the basis of all learning and behavior. This approach, sometimes referred to as S-R (stimulus-response), opened the door to a world of lab-based testing—both on humans and animals. The ground rules were clear: only what could be measured counted as data, and any guesswork about what was going on inside the head was ruled out. Behaviorists referred to the mind as a "black box" yielding no clues of its inner workings, and theories (such as Freud's) that made such claims were set aside as pure speculation.

Ivan Pavlov's experiments on conditioned responses in dogs were a key influence on the behaviorists, who saw the potential for a stimulus-response–based theory of learning across a wide range of human experience. John B. Watson went so far as to claim that under the right circumstances, behavioral techniques meant that any child could be taught anything: "Give me a dozen healthy infants, well-formed, and my own specified world to bring them up in and I'll guarantee to take any one at random and train him to become any type of specialist I might select—doctor, lawyer, artist, merchant-chief and, yes, even beggar-man and thief, regardless of his talents,

penchants, tendencies, abilities, vocations, and race of his ancestors." Emotions, too, could be conditioned through stimulus and response. Watson's 1920 experiment with "Little Albert" showed it was possible to condition fear in a baby—effectively inducing a phobia of rats in a small child through a series of lab experiments (an unthinkable procedure today, as psychology's ethical codes have evolved).

Ingenious lab tests

Burrhus Frederic (known universally as B. F.) Skinner was a generation after Watson, and became one of the most influential behavioral psychologists of the twentieth century, from the publication of his seminal book *The Behavior of Organisms* in 1938 until his retirement from Harvard in 1974. He performed lab tests of great ingenuity, often involving his "operant conditioning chamber" (or the Skinner Box)—a closed chamber containing various mechanisms designed to study the behavior of pigeons, rats, and other creatures. Unlike Pavlov's "classical conditioning," which showed how pairing different stimuli can alter behaviors, operant conditioning studies the way in which the consequences of an action influence learning. Skinner found that positive outcomes were more influential on behavior than negative stimuli —a finding that had far-reaching implications for learning and teaching. He even applied behaviorist ideas to the acquisition of language with his 1957 book *Verbal Behavior*.

However, by the 1950s, despite the undoubted experimental breakthroughs, the behavioral approach had increasing numbers of critics. If, for example, we are influenced by the consequences of an action, what part is played by how we understand those consequences? And if all behavior is the result of stimulus-response, then do we really have free will?

COGNITIVE PSYCHOLOGY

Cognitive psychology is about what happens inside that "black box" of the brain. It grew up out of several scientific disciplines that were all emerging around the middle of the twentieth century: neuroscience, linguistics, and information processing, with its links to the new science of computing. In essence, it rejected both behaviorism—for *not* taking into account the thinking processes that go on inside our heads—and psychoanalysis, for *only* taking into account the internal models of the mind at the exclusion of experimental evidence and so much other human experience.

Cognitive psychology was therefore guaranteed to upset the maximum number of apple carts. Not surprisingly, its emergence is often referred to as the cognitive "revolution" and this is perhaps how it felt in the United States, where behavioral psychology held more sway over university departments than, say, in Western Europe. In Vienna, Austria, Jean Piaget and his team were looking at learning acquisition, thought, language, and so on from as early as the 1920s, through to the 1950s and beyond. In Moscow, Lev Vygotsky was exploring the social aspects behind the acquisition of learning in the 1920s and 1930s (although his work was not translated into English until the 1960s, by which time it found favor with the new cognitive movement). But while Piaget and Vygotsky were early pioneers in Europe, the revolution in America took off in the 1950s when linguistics theorist Noam Chomsky famously demolished the behaviorists' view of language acquisition. The cognitive movement continued to gain ground, with the Harvard Center for Cognitive Studies opening in 1960, and Ulric Neisser's influential book *Cognitive Psychology* appearing in 1967.

Making sense of it all

The cognitive approach draws together a number of related fields. These can be broadly categorized as perception of the world around us from the information we pick up from our senses; our representation of knowledge through concepts, categories, and symbols; all aspects of language and memory; and such everyday thinking activities as making decisions, understanding numbers, and working things out. It is a vast field, with applications that include education, understanding memory and treating memory disorders, accident prevention, advertising and marketing, product design, control systems and user experience, military applications, the medical treatment of mental disorders (most notably with what has become Cognitive Behavioral Therapy)—and almost every aspect of learning. This, as we shall see later in this book, marked a major departure from the psychoanalytic therapy model, which attributes depression or anxiety to unpleasant events in the past. Instead, as first Albert Ellis and then Aaron T. Beck showed, it can be the irrational thoughts triggered by such events that drive us into depression: in other words, it is partly about how we make sense of the world, rather than what has actually happened, been remembered, or repressed.

A vast terrain

Today's cognitive psychologists are split into three main camps: there are the experimental psychologists, working with human participants; the information-processing branch, which is about algorithms, math, and artificial intelligence; and the neuroscientific work, using sophisticated imaging technology to track how different parts of the brain fire up, for how long, and in what sequence, as we perform various tasks.

At first cognitive psychology appeared rooted to laboratory-based experiments that could seem a long way from real world situations—and thus lacking in "ecological validity," to use the technical term. Similarly, if you only consider psychology from an information-processing perspective, it is easy to overlook the social and emotional aspects. Aware of these limitations, cognitive psychologists quickly expanded beyond the confines of the lab to explore how people understand their surroundings, with fascinating insights into the social context in which we all live and breathe.

HUMANISTIC PSYCHOLOGY

As we have seen, the move toward cognitive psychology came about through frustrations with what were seen as the limitations of psychoanalysis and behavioral psychology. In the 1950s, another movement within psychology also began to gain ground—one that rejected all the main strands of psychology: psychoanalysis, behavioral psychology, and the emerging cognitive psychology approach. This fourth approach has become known as humanistic psychology. Rather than seeing the human psyche as a minefield of conflicting parts of the self, driven by primitive urges (as the psychoanalytic approach was characterized), or viewing the self as the result of myriad stimulus-response exchanges that make us who we are (as behaviorists do), or seeing the reasons for our beliefs and actions as residing in our perception and cognition of what's around us (as the cognitive psychologists are doing), humanist psychologists view the individual as a whole person with their own free will, desires, responsibilities, passions, aims, and aspirations. In short, all the kinds of things that make us human. For the humanists, the concept of mental health for too long had been obsessed with reducing negative states such as anxiety or depression. The humanists wanted mental health to be all about striving for something better, like happiness or fulfillment.

What do you really want from life?

Two key thinkers are the pioneers of the humanist psychology movement. One is Abraham Maslow, best known for his 1954 concept of the "hierarchy of needs," which dates from 1943, and which presents an image of what people really want from life—and the idea of striving for something for its own sake. Having established lower-order needs—such as food, shelter, belonging, self-esteem—we seek knowledge, meaning, and, ultimately, the realization of our full potential. The second, Carl Rogers, shared Maslow's view that humankind seeks this higher state of self-actualization, making the most of our talents or education or skills. And along with that, we seek positive regard, which can be love, or simply respect, from others. In his 1961 book *On Becoming a Person*, he discussed some of the conditions necessary to achieve this state—a discussion that was to form the basis of a client-centered therapy (later renamed "person-centered" therapy). At its heart is the concept of unconditional positive regard—the kind of parental love that children can enjoy no matter what they might do, and which gives them a freedom to take risks and discover what they like doing. In cases where children receive only *conditional* positive regard, parental love may only be won through good behavior or excellent performance, with the risks of the child becoming a perfectionist or neurotic later in life. Client-centered therapy could redress this by the therapist providing the unconditional positive regard, and allowing the client to start finding their own way toward their self-actualizing goals.

The "I" and the "me"

For Rogers, an important theoretical aspect was the self concept. There are two parts to it: the "I" that does stuff, and the "me" that the "I" sometimes thinks about, such as when we say "I am ashamed of myself." The self concept develops as we grow up, and we are happiest, Rogers believed, when we have congruence between the "I" and the "me"—that is, minimal conflict between the perceived self and the kind of behaviors we actually find ourselves doing. Rogers developed his "Q Sort" test—a kind of personality test using a deck of flash cards—to measure levels of this congruence, which allowed for some degree of quantitative testing to demonstrate correlation between congruence of the self concept, and other measures of well-being or social adjustment.

Nonetheless, humanistic psychology is often characterized as being more of a qualitative than quantitative strand of psychology. By contrast, positive psychology is a related branch that also has as its goal not simply a reduction of psychological pain, but more positively, the advancement of well-being—looking, for example, at the science of happiness, or how creativity is stimulated: in many respects, another route to the summit of Maslow's hierarchy of needs.

TIMELINE

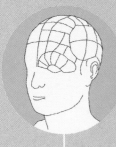

PSYCHOANALYSIS
Sigmund Freud publishes *Interpretation of Dreams*, outlining his theory of the unconscious; he develops his psychoanalytic theory for the following three decades. Meanwhile, the new field of psychoanalysis diversifies, with Carl Jung developing his own area of analytical psychology.

LEARNING
Jean Piaget publishes *The Moral Judgment of the Child*. He, and many other European thinkers, takes a different tack from the mainly US-based behaviorists, theorizing about how our minds make sense of the world, and foreshadowing the emergence of cognitive psychology twenty years later.

1879 — **1899** — **1913** — **1932**

BEGINNINGS
The first experimental lab for psychology research is set up by Wilhelm Wundt in the University of Leipzig; Hermann Ebbinghaus publishes his major work on memory six years later. Around the same time in the United States, Johns Hopkins University opens a psychology lab and William James's *Principles of Psychology* is published. Psychology, as a discipline, is up and running.

BEHAVIORISM
A totally different path from that of Freud emerges, with John B. Watson's lecture "Psychology as the Behaviorist Views It." Human behavior can be studied in the same way as that of animals: as responses to stimuli, and adaptation to the environment.

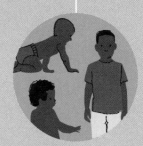

THERAPY
The Harvard Center for Cognitive Studies opens, reflecting the growing international importance of the "new" cognitive psychology. In 1967, Aaron T. Beck publishes his game-changing book on depression, linking the illness to distorted beliefs and "automatic thoughts." Beck goes on to create Cognitive Behavioral Therapy.

INFLUENCE
The Nobel Prize in Economic Sciences is awarded to a psychologist, Daniel Kahneman, for his research on decision-making in conditions of uncertainty—a reflection of the reach and influence of the discipline of psychology today.

 1952 **1960** **1971** **2002**

DEFINITIONS
The first DSM (*Diagnostic and Statistical Manual of Mental Disorders*) is published, which sets out to define what is meant by mental ill-health. Revised periodically, its fifth edition is published in 2013.

SOCIETY
Philip Zimbardo's Stanford "Prison" Experiment shows the extent to which our actions and behavior can be influenced by the society around us and the roles we play—following on from Stanley Milgram's obedience experiments. Social psychology, which had been growing in importance for the previous decade, grabs public imagination. And the ethical dimension of psychological experimentation takes center stage.

"The propensity
to make strong
emotional bonds to
particular individuals
is a basic component
of human nature."

JOHN BOWLBY,
A SECURE BASE (1988)

1
DEVELOPMENT & LANGUAGE

INTRODUCTION

Before launching into the first chapter of this book, let's think for a moment about the first chapter of each of our own lives. How did we get from that first day—our birth day—to where we are now? One of the missions of psychology is to try to answer this question. And one of the first people to do this in a systematic and theoretical way was Sigmund Freud. Broadly speaking, Freud believed that the most critical developmental challenge for every child is to negotiate the shift from being within an exclusive two-person relationship (mother and child), to realizing that they must share their mother with her own partner, with whom she has another kind of exclusive relationship. This is at the heart of Freud's Oedipus Complex, which he believed brought with it a range of anxieties, jealousies, and even murderous fantasies (which we needn't go into here) that would have a bearing on a person's development later in life. Freud's psychoanalytic theory of development can be seen as a starting point for a century of theory, research, and debate on how it is that we become our "selves"—and how we then go on to learn and develop as distinct individuals.

Attachment and beyond

We start off with the idea of attachment. Mary Ainsworth's "strange situation" test (pages 26–27) involves leaving a small child alone in an unfamiliar room, and is something that anyone who has ever met a toddler can instantly relate to. It proved to be of crucial importance to researchers, providing an ingenious kind of objective yardstick against which to measure the behavior of infants, and opening up an entire field of experimental psychology.

John Bowlby (pages 28–29) is the pioneer of work that became known as "attachment theory," and in this chapter we look at one of his early studies, "Forty-four Juvenile Thieves: Their Characters and Home Life," which began to explore how early attachment failures can affect later behavior. The topic was a pressing one, with World War II displacing millions of young people, many of them orphaned, across the world.

From the 1930s to the 1960s, many psychology experiments used animals, such was the prevalence of the "behavioral" psychology tradition, which held that we, like other animals, are physically programmed to behave in a certain way: feeding, for example, will lead to attachment. Harry Harlow's experiments with monkeys (pages 30–31), however, showed that attachment to their mother was about more than craving food. The baby monkeys seemed to crave nurturing care even more than food, and an absence of this care would cause symptoms of depression and withdrawal.

Learning about learning

This first chapter also takes a look at the theory of how we learn—starting with Ivan Pavlov's famous experiments on his laboratory dogs (pages 32–33), which influenced generations of research on the learning and unlearning process. Thinking about learning throws up some interesting questions. Does our ability to learn and understand increasingly complex material simply depend on the physical development of our brains? Jean Piaget, watching his three clever children growing up, thought it probably did (pages 34–35). In a similar way, Lawrence Kohlberg (pages 42–43) believed that our moral senses also simply evolve with age. Others, like Lev Vygotsky, in revolutionary Russia, believed that the society around us was an essential component of learning (pages 36–37). Not that learning is something that is confined to children, of course. Erik Erikson (pages 38–39) saw life as containing a series of eight distinct "crises" to be negotiated at various stages, each with far-reaching consequences.

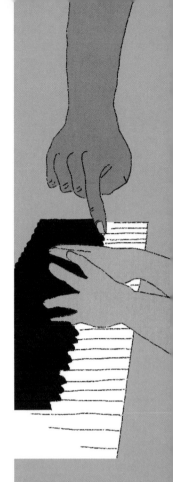

The mechanisms of learning are explored, too. Albert Bandura's ideas on learning through imitation of others (pages 40–41) may seem rather obvious today, but at the time they were revolutionary, challenging the behaviorist principles that suggest learning is only driven by incentives—sticks and carrots. In a similar way, Noam Chomsky comprehensively rubbished the behaviorist idea that we learn a language by trial and error. However, his alternative (pages 44–45)—that we all possess the innate ability to learn a language—today appears a rather extreme alternative: it would appear that we still need some kind of teaching.

We offer two very different reflections on gender. Simon Baron-Cohen's work on autism (pages 46–47) has pointed out some significant differences between the functioning of male and female brains, based on what men and women appear to be "good at." Returning to the learning theme, our second topic on gender identity (pages 48–49) shows how far gender can be tied to the expectations of our social environment: gender as something we do, rather than something we are.

Finally, we take a look at the work of Carol Dweck and others on the kind of mindset that can help people push to achieve more, which comes down to how we view the nature of the task, and our capacity to learn (pages 50–51). If you fall into a category of people who believe that learning capacity can be continually expanded, then read on!

BIOGRAPHIES

JEAN PIAGET (1896–1980)

Piaget was born in Neuchâtel, Switzerland. Precociously bright, he idolized his academic father and quickly developed a boyhood passion for natural history, publishing a short paper on an albino sparrow when he was just age ten, and yet more papers on mollusks in his teens. He completed a Ph.D. in zoology and philosophy in 1918, but it was when working with Theodore Simon in 1920 on children's intelligence tests that his contribution to psychology sparked into life. Piaget noticed how, in their answers, children made certain kinds of errors, depending on their age, and this led to a quest to discover how children acquire understanding. As professor of child psychology at the University of Geneva (where he remained for the rest of his career), Piaget developed sophisticated techniques for interviewing children (often his own three) about how they think. He then evolved his four-stage theory of learning, where a child uses "schemas" to make sense of the world around them, then adapts or replaces them when new explanations fit better. As Piaget famously said: "What we know changes what we see. What we see changes what we know." Piaget's ideas sparked new thinking in the area of education and curriculum development, with the notion that children learn best when the approach fits their capacity to think.

JOHN BOWLBY (1907–1990)

Bowlby was the pioneer of attachment theory, which explores the emotional bond between a child and their caregiver, and what happens when that bond is broken. Bowlby's family was well-off (his father was surgeon to the royal household) and much of his early care was consigned to nannies. He later recalled his pain when one nanny left the job—he described it as like losing a mother. Bowlby was sent to boarding school at age ten, and later graduated from Cambridge (in psychology) and London University (in medicine), then qualified as a psychoanalyst specializing in children. His work in the late 1930s at a London school for "maladjusted" children convinced him that family experiences were crucial to the mental health of young people (rather than internal mental conflicts, as psychoanalysts believed). After the war he set up a research unit at the Tavistock Institute, where he became director of child psychiatry. Bowlby's theories on attachment gained global interest with the publication of his report on homeless children, commissioned by the World Health Organization. His theory was published in book form in three major works: *Attachment* (1969), *Separation* (1973), and *Loss* (1980). A further influential work, *A Secure Base*, was published in 1988.

MARY AINSWORTH (1913–1999)

Ainsworth introduced detailed techniques of infant observation and assessment to mainstream psychology. She graduated from the University of Toronto, and her choice of doctorate (completed 1939) presaged her future celebrated career: it explored "security theory," the idea that infants need secure dependence on parents, or a secure base, before going into unfamiliar situations. After World War II she taught courses on personality assessment and co-authored a book on the Rorschach inkblot test, then moved to London in 1950, joining Bowlby's research unit for three years and exploring the effects on children of separation from their mother. Struck by how relevant Bowlby's theories appeared to be, she set out to collect evidence of infant–mother interactions with observational studies—first in Uganda, and later back in the United States, while working as a lecturer at Johns Hopkins University. This work involved unprecedented levels of study, involving home visits to dozens of families, gathering over 1,000 hours of data on mother–child interactions. Ainsworth also developed the "strange situation" observational technique, published in book form in 1978. She moved to the University of Virginia in 1975, and continued working in the field of mother–infant attachment into her seventies.

ALBERT BANDURA (1925–)

Bandura was brought up on a remote farm in Canada, attending a local school with just two teachers and very few textbooks, but his passion for self-directed learning earned him a place at the University of British Columbia, then a Ph.D. from the University of Iowa, after which he took up a teaching role at Stanford in 1953, where he remains as emeritus professor. While best known for the "Bobo doll" experiment, which showed how children will copy adult behavior, he is most celebrated for his pioneering "social cognitive theory," of which the Bobo doll evidence was just one small part. This theory holds that our actions are influenced by a cocktail of social, cognitive, and behavioral factors all at once—rather than a single dominant factor, as mainstream psychology had previously believed. This groundbreaking shift away from behavioral psychology had huge implications for education and social policy. Bandura has since expanded the theory into further areas: research on "mastery" (how people learn), social persuasion and how it can encourage behavior, and the factors affecting people's ability to self-regulate. Bandura's book *Moral Disengagement: How People Do Harm and Live With Themselves*, was published when he was 90.

AINSWORTH & ATTACHMENT

THE MAIN CONCEPT | Small babies are pretty easygoing when it comes to dealing with strangers. Then, after about seven months, they become much more attached to their primary caregiver and start to show signs of anxiety at times of separation, however brief. Studying such separations—and reunions—provides a window into the strength and nature of infant attachments, and in the field of developmental psychology, led to what's known as the "strange situation" test (see opposite). Devised by Mary Ainsworth and colleagues in the 1970s, this collected a huge amount of data on mother–infant interactions, and led to the characterization of attachment patterns into three categories: "avoidant," "secure," and "ambivalent." Ainsworth found that a child's attachment style was closely linked to how sensitive a mother was in responding to her child's needs, a conclusion based on detailed and systematic observations of infants with their mothers in Baltimore, where Ainsworth gathered more than 70 hours of observational data from 26 newborn babies. Mothers who avoided bodily contact with their infants, or whose care was inconsistent, tended to have babies who developed avoidant and ambivalent attachment. By contrast, mothers who understood their infant's perspective—and who were accessible, cooperative, and consistent in their care, tended to have babies who formed secure attachments.

MARY AINSWORTH BIOGRAPHY
Page 25

BOWLBY & DEPRIVATION
Page 28

HARLOW'S MONKEYS
Page 30

THE EVIDENCE | In Ainsworth's "strange situation" procedure a mother and baby enter a room containing toys, and the mother lets the baby explore. A female stranger enters, talks to the mother, then approaches the baby. The mother goes out briefly, the stranger plays with the baby, and the mother returns and settles the baby. At the end of the experiment, after a second exit by the mother, she returns, greets the baby, and picks them up. The baby's reactions—to the unfamiliar room, to the stranger, to the mother's leaving and especially to her return—all provide vital clues to their attachment style. A "securely attached" baby, for example, will be distressed when their mother leaves and happy when she returns, while an "anxious/avoidant" baby will show little interest in either.

THE WIDER PICTURE | *Are children's attachments to their primary caregiver or parents set in stone? Or can they change— moving from insecure, say, to secure? The bulk of research following in the footsteps of Ainsworth's work suggests that a child's attachment type is fluid, and will be formed and re-formed by the ever-changing patterns of relationships and events within their family unit as they grow up.*

BOWLBY & DEPRIVATION

THE MAIN CONCEPT | "This child is depraved on account he ain't had a normal home." In this line from the musical *West Side Story*, written in 1957, we can see some cutting-edge thinking in psychology taking, quite literally, center stage. The idea that deprivation could affect children's mental well-being was a hot topic in the 1950s, and owed much to the work of John Bowlby, who became convinced that babies strive for social contact, and that this was an essential part of their developmental process. The issue became an important one in the years following the end of World War II, with hundreds of thousands of orphaned and displaced children spread across Europe, Asia, and the United States, many living in institutions or with foster carers. In 1950 Bowlby was commissioned by the World Health Organization to investigate the effects of a broken maternal bond on young children. His conclusion, based on extensive research, was that the first three years of life were crucial, and that to ensure healthy mental development "the infant and young child should experience a warm, intimate, and continuous relationship with his mother (or permanent mother substitute) in which both find satisfaction and enjoyment." This, he believed, provides an internal "model" for the child to understand themselves and others, forming a blueprint for expectations and behaviors in future relationships.

THE EVIDENCE | In 1944 John Bowlby published a paper entitled "Forty-four Juvenile Thieves: Their Characters and Home-Life," which examined the experiences of 88 children and teens referred to a specialist mental health clinic in London. Half the group were nondeliquents, while the other half made up the 44 "thieves." Among the various character types represented, what stood out was an extremely troubled group that Bowlby termed "affectionless psychopaths." Almost every member of this group had been stealing persistently. Bowlby found similarities in their personalities, and "a remarkably distinctive early history—prolonged separation from their mothers or foster mothers." He described this as "an unusually clear example of the distorting influence of a bad early environment upon the development of personality."

THE WIDER PICTURE | *Postwar research into maternal deprivation sparked controversy, and the findings were quickly seized upon by those promoting the merits of stay-at-home mothers. Later research, however, added balance: Michael Rutter's 1981* Maternal Deprivation Reassessed *found that the effects of maternal deprivation had more to do with the quality of a child's relationships and experiences than simply the presence or absence of the mother.*

JOHN BOWLBY BIOGRAPHY
Page 24
AINSWORTH & ATTACHMENT
Page 26
HARLOW'S MONKEYS
Page 30

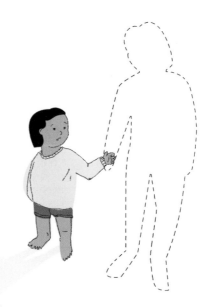

HARLOW'S MONKEYS

THE MAIN CONCEPT | Should a crying baby simply be
left unattended until the next feeding time? In the first
half of the twentieth century, the prevailing view was that
a baby's attachment to its mother was simply about
satisfying hunger. Therefore, according to behavioral
psychologists—led by John B. Watson—infants should be
left to cry in between feeds; picking them up for caresses
and cuddles would simply spoil them and make them
overdependent. As a result, in homes, nurseries, maternity
units, and in hospitals and orphanages, human contact
with young babies was rationed, which today seems cruel
and ludicrous. The change in thinking is in part thanks
to attachment theorists including John Bowlby and Mary
Ainsworth, and to animal behavior research by Harry
Harlow. For obvious ethical reasons, psychologists could
not simply deprive a human infant of its mother and study
the consequences. However, in the 1950s, doing this kind
of work with primates was possible, and Harlow began a
series of experiments with baby rhesus monkeys at the
University of Wisconsin. His key finding was that infant
primates needed comfort as much as they needed food,
and that a lack of social contact would have long-lasting
negative consequences, including the fact that these
monkeys would be less likely to act as competent parents
when they produced offspring of their own.

THE EVIDENCE | Harlow set up his own lab where he raised rhesus monkeys in isolation from each other. Inside their cages were crude models that dispensed milk—"surrogate mothers" with a body, head, and face, either made from a hard wire frame, or covered with soft terry cloth. The monkeys preferred to feed from the cloth model, and showed signs of a growing attachment to it: even when the cloth "mother" did not dispense milk, they still ran to it to seek comfort at times of alarm or stress—for example, when Harlow introduced into the cage a clockwork bear that would walk around beating a drum.

AINSWORTH & ATTACHMENT
Page 26

BOWLBY & DEPRIVATION
Page 28

SELIGMAN & DEPRESSION
Page 138

THE WIDER PICTURE | *Harlow's experiments showed that infant monkeys have an underlying need for the comfort of contact. Although applying findings from animal studies to humans is often questionable, the key takeaway here is that comfort—and thus the fulfillment of emotional needs—rather than just the provision of food, is a key condition to the formation of attachments and healthy mental development.*

PAVLOV & CLASSICAL CONDITIONING

THE MAIN CONCEPT | There can be no dogs more famous in the history of psychology than those belonging to Russian physiologist Ivan Pavlov. Pavlov's experiments on his dogs (see opposite) are all the more appealing because of their simplicity: dogs were trained to associate the sound of a buzzer with getting their dinner, so when they heard the buzzer, they salivated. Why, though, is this experiment so famous, and why was it seen as such a breakthrough? Already a Nobel Prize winner (in 1904) for his work on the physiology of digestion, Pavlov came upon the phenomenon of conditioned reflexes during his experimental work on dogs' digestive systems. His experiments showed that it was possible for the dogs to learn (and unlearn) automatic responses to new stimuli, a phenomenon known as a "conditioned reflex." They led to widespread work on what became known as "classical conditioning"—to see how far these learned responses could be observed in other animals as well as in humans. Pavlov's work came at an opportune time, reinforcing the prevailing view that the observable stimulus and response were the pure building blocks of everything that could be studied by psychology—the foundations of the behavioral approach. Even a century later, Pavlov's physiological approach and concept of the conditioned reflex remains relevant, most notably in neuroscientific research into the effects of post-traumatic stress disorder.

THE EVIDENCE | Pavlov had observed how his laboratory dogs would start salivating when they heard the approaching footsteps of the person bringing their food. He then tried to teach the dogs to link other, unrelated, stimuli (such as a buzzer) with this salivating response, by pairing those stimuli with the food. He began by repeatedly presenting the food to a dog right after a buzzer was heard. He then put a dog in a harness and used a tube to capture and measure its saliva. Soon enough, upon the sound of the buzzer, the dog salivated. Further experiments showed how such effects could be unlearned and relearned, as well as how the dogs could learn to distinguish different or similar sounds.

THE WIDER PICTURE | *Pavlov's discoveries have had far-reaching effects, and have been influential on many aspects of behavioral therapy, not least in the treatment of phobias, where exposure therapy can extinguish the conditioned reflex—the phobic fear. He is also present, invisibly, in many classroom situations, as teachers strive to deal with learning "phobias"—aiming to link learning with positive emotions and to reduce anxiety.*

BEHAVIORAL PSYCHOLOGY
Page 12

HARD GRAFT OR GENIUS?
Page 132

SELIGMAN & DEPRESSION
Page 138

PIAGET & LEARNING

THE MAIN CONCEPT | What really goes on inside the newly minted mind of a small baby, and how do they get from there to becoming smart young adults? In 1936, Swiss biologist Jean Piaget proposed a sophisticated theory of cognitive development, based on extensive observations of children at play. He came up with the idea of mental "schemas," which, roughly speaking, are a child's idea of how the world around it works. The most basic is the "body schema," or how a baby learns to distinguish between itself and everything else: the "me" and the "not me." Babies start off totally egocentric—for example, if they can't see an object, they don't think it is there (see opposite). As time goes on, this diminishes, as children eventually start to see that objects have an independent existence, and later, that other people have a distinct and separate existence, as well as a distinct view of the world. Development happens as the child discards schemas and adopts new ones in line with its interactions with (or "operations on," as Piaget puts it) its environment. Piaget described four stages of child development: "sensorimotor" (age 0–2), "pre-operational" (2–7), "concrete operational" (7–11) , and "formal operational" (11 and up), by which time children, he thought, were acquiring adult-level capacities for abstract thought and logical reasoning.

THE EVIDENCE | Piaget drew on a vast array of play-based observations—often with his own children. Here is one example. A baby is playing with a toy and the experimenter drops a cloth over the toy. The baby stops trying to find it because, according to Piaget, it thinks it no longer exists. At about nine months old, however, there is a subtle change, and the baby will reach repeatedly for a toy that is concealed in front of it. But if the toy is then hidden (in full view of the baby) in a different place, the baby will carry on reaching for it in the initial location. This is because at this "egocentric" stage, the baby thinks the existence of the toy is part of its act of reaching out for it.

THE WIDER PICTURE | *Piaget's work (especially his notion of schemas) was highly influential in the evolving science of cognitive development. As time went on, however, his experimental evidence was widely challenged, and from the 1960s onward, the weak point in his theory was exposed: the prominent role of social interaction in learning and development—which Piaget largely ignored.*

JEAN PIAGET BIOGRAPHY
Page 24

VYGOTSKY & LEARNING
Page 36

BANDURA & SOCIAL LEARNING
Page 40

VYGOTSKY & LEARNING

THE MAIN CONCEPT | If you get the chance to watch four-year-olds at play, you'll notice how much they talk to themselves, especially when they are getting involved in a complicated task. What do we make of this? The psychologist Jean Piaget (pages 34–35) thought that such speech was a sign of a developmental stage not yet being reached—a failure to be able to converse openly with others. The Soviet psychologist Lev Vygotsky held a different view—that in fact this private talk was an essential stage in mental development, and was a direct route to internal speech and thought, and adult thought processes. This difference of opinion reflected two vastly different models of the mind. For Piaget, a child's mental development was a physical maturing process as it made sense of the world around it. But for Vygotsky, a child's learning was totally dependent on and shaped by the society and culture around it—it was a social process, leading to the acquisition of language, which led on to the ability to process internal language and rational thought. Crucially, he believed that children could not learn without a "more knowledgeable other" to guide them, showing them how to put names to objects, and later how to accomplish things they could do on their own, providing a kind of scaffolding while the child built its learning.

THE EVIDENCE | Vygotsky's collaborator Rosa Levina carried out a series of studies in which she observed children's speech during play activities. In one study, Levina challenged a four-year-old girl to retrieve sweets from a high shelf, using a stool and a stick as her only tools. As the girl became more involved in the task, she began to talk to herself. Standing on the stool, she said: "On the stool." Feeling along the shelf with a stick, she said: "Is that really the sweets? I can get them with the other stool." Then, positioning another stool: "No that doesn't get it, I can use the stick." Vygotsky found this kind of private speech became less common as children got slightly older. In his view, it went "underground"—becoming the basis of our inner thought processes.

THE WIDER PICTURE | *The key social dimension to children's cognitive development was Vygotsky's attempt at a kind of Marxist version of developmental psychology—he lived, after all, in 1920s Russia. The idea got parked for 30 years after his premature death in 1934, but since the 1960s it has linked well with Western cognitive and social approaches to the subject, and his theories on teaching and learning have been taken up by educationalists worldwide.*

PIAGET & LEARNING
Page 34
BANDURA & SOCIAL LEARNING
Page 40
CHOMSKY & LANGUAGE
Page 44

ERIKSON'S EIGHT STAGES OF MAN

THE MAIN CONCEPT | When we talk about "growing up," we usually have in mind the 20 or so years between being born and becoming an adult. We tend not to think of growing up as something that never ceases. But in 1950, German-born psychoanalyst Erik Erikson, then at the University of California, published *Childhood and Society*, a book in which he proposed that our personalities continue to develop throughout our lives, from infancy right through to extreme old age. Erikson identified eight "stages of man," each characterized by what he called a "psychosocial crisis" between the developing self and the demands posed by personal and social surroundings. From the young infant's struggle to develop trust, the older infant strives for a sense of autonomy, and later, responsibility. In the early school years, the battle is for competence versus feelings of inferiority. Later still, adolescents are seeking their adult identity, but struggling with role confusion—the identity crisis. In young adulthood, the conflict is between the risks of intimacy versus retreat into isolation. Fast forward to middle age and the "task" is to fulfill our life goals. How we fare on that front can lead to a sense either of productivity or stagnation. Finally, in our old age, as we try to make sense of what we are left with, we face a final battle between integrity and despair.

THE EVIDENCE | Erikson developed his theory through an eclectic mix of research and observational methods, which included clinical interviews, observations of children taking part in play therapy, questionnaires, analysis of literary works and the biographies of famous people, and anthropological fieldwork, including testing his eight-stage model on members of two Native American tribes—the Oglala Sioux and the Yurok. However, there has also been a wealth of research based on his stage theory, and it has been widely vindicated in particular as a framework through which to view the challenges of adult life (see below). Much research has been based on questionnaires, while American psychiatrist George Vaillant is noted for carrying out longitudinal studies that have followed the same participants through decades of their lives.

THE WIDER PICTURE | *Erikson's theory showed how our capacity for change and development continues after the first 20 years of our lives, right through to the very end. It provided a new framework for thinking about the problems of adults as they seek therapeutic interventions—and helped to shed light on the psychological challenges facing the very oldest people in our communities.*

PSYCHOANALYSIS
Page 10

VYGOTSKY & LEARNING
Page 36

KOHLBERG & MORALITY
Page 42

BANDURA & SOCIAL LEARNING

THE MAIN CONCEPT | Does watching violence make us act violently? The ancient Greeks asked themselves this question, and it is still asked in today's world of TV and social media. The quick answer is "yes," but only slightly, given that there are dozens of other factors that affect whether we act violently or not. But in the 1950s, as TV sets began to enter every home and violent shows drew large audiences, the question was a hot topic among researchers. Until then, the answers had been drawn from some very established thinkers. Psychoanalysts, following Freud, believed anger came from an aggressive drive that was within all of us. Aggressive kids were simply letting this out in a healthy way, and for adults, watching boxing matches or violent movies helped "drain" the aggressive drive—a process Freud called catharsis. Behavioral psychologists also thought violent TV was harmless: followers of B. F. Skinner and John B. Watson believed that behaviors were learned through repeated stimulus, trial and error, or incentives like positive or negative outcomes—copying just didn't come into it. Or did it? Albert Bandura, however, turned conventional wisdom upside-down with his "Bobo doll" experiments (see opposite), which refocused the theory of learning to incorporate the crucial processes of observation, imitation, and identification.

THE EVIDENCE | In the famous Bobo doll experiment, conducted in 1961 at Stanford University, nursery school children were shown a film of an adult performing aggressive acts on an inflatable clown—called Bobo—while making aggressive remarks. Bandura, Dorothea Ross, and Sheila Ross then modeled the levels of aggression the children had learned while watching the film. They found that children who did not watch the film, or who watched a film showing gentle play with the Bobo doll did not play aggressively, while those who had watched the aggressive version copied it, and even showed greater inclination to play with toy weapons such as a gun or a hammer and beat up the toy clown.

THE WIDER PICTURE | *Up to the 1960s, psychologists still strongly believed that learning was led by incentives—sticks and carrots—and by trial and error. After this time, there was a sea change in thinking, with the realization that effective and rapid learning could occur via imitation alone, with positive attitudes to a specific role model playing a key part. This has had a profound effect on many aspects of our lives, including how schoolteachers teach.*

ALBERT BANDURA BIOGRAPHY
Page 25
VYGOTSKY & LEARNING
Page 36
WORK IN PROGRESS
Page 128

KOHLBERG & MORALITY

THE MAIN CONCEPT | Here is a story of two girls. One wanted to give her mom a surprise by doing some sewing for her, but accidentally cut a big hole in her dress. The other girl played with scissors when her mom was out and accidentally cut a small hole in her dress. Which of the two deserves the biggest punishment? When Swiss psychologist Jean Piaget (pages 34–35) asked children this question in the 1930s, he found that younger children thought cutting the bigger hole deserved a bigger punishment. But for older children, the good intention of the first girl merited a smaller punishment. Observations like these resulted in a theory of moral development based on stages of understanding as children grow up. Three decades later, Lawrence Kohlberg proposed six stages of moral development, also based on researching children's views on various scenarios. The stages were grouped into three levels, starting with "pre-moral" stages, where children are most concerned with obedience to rules. Next came "conventionally moral" stages, influenced by the social consensus; here, good intentions play a part, and eventually, so does a sense of whether an act is good or bad for society. In the most advanced stage— "autonomous morality"—teenagers notice that there are differing moral views within society, and begin to work out their own generalized sense of right and wrong.

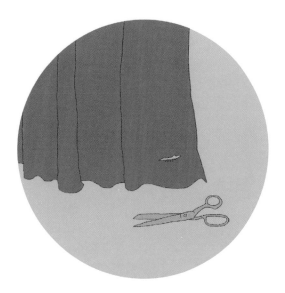

PIAGET & LEARNING
Page 34

VYGOTSKY & LEARNING
Page 36

BANDURA & SOCIAL LEARNING
Page 40

THE EVIDENCE | Kohlberg's most famous scenario is that of a man called Heinz, whose wife is dying from cancer and who is unable to buy her medication because the pharmacist is charging too much, so Heinz breaks into the pharmacy to steal the drugs. The stages of moral development emerge clearly in discussing the case. Pre-moral opinions come out as: "He might get caught and be punished." Conventional morality is expressed with statements like: "People will think he's a thief." The higher level autonomous morality can be seen in comments such as: "The pharmacist is wrong to charge so much, but we have to respect each other's rights, and it would be wrong to steal the drugs."

THE WIDER PICTURE | *Later studies by Judith Smetana demonstrated that children as young as four can sense the greater seriousness of moral transgressions (such as aggression), compared with ordinary rule-breaking, such as not going to bed on time—even if they are told off in the same way for both kinds of misdeed. Somehow, children seem to figure out basic morality from their social surroundings earlier than traditional stage theories would predict.*

CHOMSKY & LANGUAGE

THE MAIN CONCEPT | How do babies acquire language? In 1957, B. F. Skinner, one of the leading behavioral psychologists of the era, published a controversial book on language acquisition that suggested it was all down to trial and error. Babies babble all kinds of sounds, happen upon something sounding like a word, and get rewarded with smiles and attention from their parents. This continues with other words, and eventually sentences, with the child developing as it responds to the rewards of approval and esteem. Language, then, was little more than conditioned "verbal behavior." One of Skinner's fiercest critics was the linguist Noam Chomsky, who demolished Skinner's approach in a book review, and went on to propose a radical alternative theory in its place. For Chomsky, infants have an innate, biological ability to learn language—a "language acquisition device," he called it—which would work for any language in the world, and is able to decode the deep structure of how the language should be used, beyond the surface structure of the vocab and verb rules. Chomsky and Skinner stood at two ends of the linguistic spectrum—and there are many theorists who now occupy the space between. The evidence (opposite) suggests that kids can't work out language all on their own simply by listening. Even if they do have a Chomsky-style disposition to learn, they still need to be taught.

THE EVIDENCE | Jacqueline Sachs, Barbara Bard, and Marie Johnson carried out a study in 1971 of two brothers, Jim (nearly four) and Glenn (nearly two), whose parents were deaf. The boys had almost no interaction with hearing adults, and communicated with their parents with rudimentary signs, but did not learn sign language. Despite watching a lot of TV and listening to his school playmates, Jim had not picked up the syntax of language expected at his age. For example: Adult—"Do you like to play ball?" Jim—"My mommy my house a play ball." But once he was given one-to-one interaction with an adult, he picked up the language rapidly—suggesting that an innate ability to learn is not enough. It takes teaching, too.

THE WIDER PICTURE | *Chomsky's comprehensive trashing of the behavioral theory of language acquisition can be seen as a tipping point in the new ascendancy of cognitive psychology—and he is credited as one of the founding fathers of the cognitive movement. His ideas of universal linguistic principles put new energy into linguistic research across the world.*

BEHAVIORAL PSYCHOLOGY
Page 12
COGNITIVE PSYCHOLOGY
Page 14
BANDURA & SOCIAL LEARNING
Page 40

BARON-COHEN & AUTISM

THE MAIN CONCEPT | It is common to hear various offhand comments regarding the difference between men and women—that men are logical creatures and women more emotional; that men are better at reading maps and women better at reading people's emotions. But is there any truth behind this? Simon Baron-Cohen, a clinical psychologist and director of the Autism Research Centre at the University of Cambridge, suggests there is. In 2003, he formulated a theory which assigned a "brain type"—regardless of gender—on an individual's particular ability to empathize or systematize. He found that female brains were largely geared toward empathizing—demonstrating greater sympathy and sensitivity toward others—whereas male brains tended more toward building and understanding systems and structures, and organizing things. Crucially, this fed into his research into autism and its effects on the normal development of a child's social and communication skills, both on a verbal and emotional level. Autistic tendencies are characterized by obsessive or repetitive behaviors and interests, and a strong preoccupation with finer details, such as a fixation with a particular object or process. Coupled with a lack of tools for empathy and the fact that there is a higher rate of autism in males, Baron-Cohen came to believe that autistic people have an extreme form of the "male" brain.

THE EVIDENCE | Baron-Cohen and colleagues invited male and female subjects to take part in a spatial analysis and visual design task, as well as an experiment to test their ability to interpret others' emotions and actions. This second test involved participants looking at 25 photographs of the eye region of someone expressing an emotion, and then choosing a word to describe what the person in the photo was feeling. Males performed better at the spatial analysis task, whereas females were better at matching emotions to the photos. Similar tests were conducted on patients affected by autism and Asperger's syndrome, who performed poorly in the photograph test, but better at the spatial awareness and visual design experiment—supporting Baron-Cohen's hypothesis that they were extremes of the "male" brain type.

GENDER IDENTITY
Page 48

WE'RE NOT ALWAYS LIKE THIS
Page 126

WORK IN PROGRESS
Page 128

THE WIDER PICTURE | *Baron-Cohen's systematizing-empathizing brain type theory and its application to autism has been very influential, especially in deepening our understanding of the condition, raising awareness, and increasing the effectiveness of treatment. The "male" brain aspect can be overstated, though. His experiments showed that around 17 percent of men have an "empathizing" brain, and 17 percent of women have a "systematizing" brain, with many others having a mix of both.*

GENDER IDENTITY

THE MAIN CONCEPT | We all know the first question that gets asked when a baby is born: "Is it a boy or a girl?" But what happens next? Does biology alone account for the differences we end up with between the sexes? Despite the important differences in chromosomes, the reproductive organs, and the kinds of hormones that circulate through our bodies, the overwhelming answer, in psychology, would appear to be that biology is not the whole story. There are two particular strands of thinking. One, called "bio-social," is about how the anatomical gender of a baby will set up a whole set of behaviors and expectations within the parents that will affect how it is going to be brought up—behaviors that can prove to be more influential than the biological gender characteristics themselves. Another strand of thinking is to see gender as an aspect of "social learning," where children learn what it means to be a boy or a girl from those around them. A famous experiment by Smith and Lloyd (see opposite) shows how this process kicks in right at the start of a baby's life. In effect, as a child grows up, the society around them reinforces and passes on its own entrenched ideas about gender roles.

THE EVIDENCE | British researchers Caroline Smith and Barbara Lloyd invited mothers to play with a baby that they didn't know. Four "actor babies" aged around six months were dressed in "gender appropriate" clothing, and introduced to the participating mothers with either a girl's name or a boy's. The mothers, who were filmed, interacted quite differently with the baby depending on whether they thought it was a boy or a girl. If the baby became restless, the "girl" was soothed and hushed, whereas the "boy" was picked up and stimulated. The girls were handed soft toys, while the boys were given more "active" toys, such as a rubber mallet. Smith and Lloyd concluded that there were "significant differences in the socialization of girls and boys which begin in early infancy."

THE WIDER PICTURE | *The fact that gender identity is shaped to such a large degree by society's expectations has led some—such as gender theorist Judith Butler—to see gender as something that we do (or are forced to do) rather than something that we are. The concept of the "nonbinary identity"—which is unrelated to one's biological boy-or-girl characteristics— can be seen as a means of side-stepping the social expectations of conformity.*

BANDURA & SOCIAL LEARNING
Page 40
BARON-COHEN & AUTISM
Page 46
THE BEAUTY BIAS
Page 112

ACHIEVEMENT MOTIVATION

THE MAIN CONCEPT | What makes people succeed? Is it brains, money, or something else—ambition, or perhaps more specifically, the combination of passion and resilience that psychologist Angela Duckworth referred to (in a book of the same name) as "grit"? Back in the 1950s, researchers were starting to explore the idea of "achievement motivation"—the need to achieve. From the outset, there was a sense that this was not simply some kind of internal trait that we either have or don't have. An experiment by Bernard Rosen and Roy D'Andrade in 1959 set young boys tasks to complete in front of their parents, and observed that the parents with high expectations *and* an ability to provide useful encouragement saw their kids do best. But since then, attention has shifted to the mind-set of the children themselves, rather than that of their parents. If children feel that success will come from effort, then they will put the effort in. However, if they feel that to succeed requires a certain ability (intelligence or skillfulness) then they may put in less effort if they think they don't have what it takes. Albert Bandura (pages 40–41) and fellow Stanford psychology professor Carol Dweck felt this came down to how children viewed intelligence: is it a collection of learned skills that can be built on and expanded (for example, by trying, failing, and trying again at a task), or is it a finite quantity that will be exposed as inadequate if you try something too difficult?

THE EVIDENCE | Carol Dweck and Elaine Elliot worked extensively to explore how a child's personal goals affect their patterns of achievement. Specifically, children can be seen as having learning goals, where they aim to increase their competence regardless of failure, or performance goals, where individuals seek favorable judgments of their competence and avoid negative judgments. In a 1988 study of 100 children of different abilities, Dweck and Elliot showed how all children will try harder to tackle a difficult task if it is sold to them as being about learning rather than about performance—irrespective of the level of skill that they think they possess.

THE WIDER PICTURE | *The aspect of this research that has captured the public imagination is the idea of what's become known as the flexible versus the fixed mindset: the notion of encouraging children to view their skills, capabilities, and intellect as flexible things that they can actively grow by trying new activities, rather than fixed, finite characteristics that may be exposed as inadequate.*

BANDURA & SOCIAL LEARNING
Page 40
INTELLIGENCE: A CAN OF WORMS
Page 130
HARD GRAFT OR GENIUS?
Page 132

"In real life, as well as in experiments, people can come to believe things that never really happened."

ELIZABETH LOFTUS,
EYEWITNESS TESTIMONY (1979)

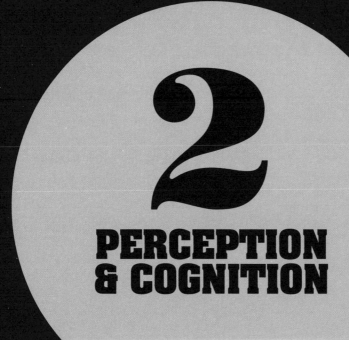

2

PERCEPTION
& COGNITION

INTRODUCTION

In this chapter we look at some of the everyday functioning of our minds—how we make sense of the world. We start with memory research, an area that has been explored since 1885 when Hermann Ebbinghaus published *Memory: A Contribution to Experimental Psychology*. His was a lab-based approach where he set out to study our ability to memorize pure information, screening out the kinds of facts that people might already know would influence the experimental outcome. He designed trigrams, made-up syllables built from three letters—a consonant, a vowel, and a consonant—that had no meaning but looked like words. Ebbinghaus and an assistant carried out these experiments on themselves, learning the trigrams from flashcards, and varying the experiments to see what factors affected their capacity to remember.

This could be called a purely cognitive approach to memory—examining the way information is processed, memorized, and recalled. The work of George A. Miller (pages 58–59) forms part of this tradition, looking at how much random information we can remember in the short term, and how we can boost our ability to remember. The problem with this kind of approach is that in real life, as we all know, we don't deal with meaningless information and there is a difference in what we remember when reading a book, tying our shoelaces, or recognizing a friend across the street.

Frederic Bartlett, another pioneer of research into memory, took a markedly different approach. Working in the 1930s, he became interested in how we organize our memories to fit in with things that we already know. Bartlett discovered that we adjust the material we hear so that it makes sense, deciding what to leave in and what to omit. His approach was more about how memory is adjusted in the light of human experience, and we can see parallels with this approach in some of the topics in this chapter, from Freud's theories about repression and the unconscious (pages 60–61), to Elizabeth Loftus's research on eyewitness testimony (pages 62–63).

Stubborn beliefs

Perception and cognition relate to what we take in from the world around us and what we make of it. While memory can seem a surprisingly slippery concept, so are the beliefs we hold—or think we hold. Faced with beliefs that clash—known as "cognitive dissonance" (pages 64–65)—we can end up unconsciously tweaking our beliefs, as if to restore order. There is a stubborn aspect to our belief systems, too. The concept of "confirmation bias" (pages 82–83) looks at how resistant we can be to information that conflicts with our most firmly held beliefs, and how this is even more marked when we are part of a like-minded group—for example on social media. And while we may claim to try to understand other people's points of view, our default position, as Lee Ross's "Fundamental Attribution Error" demonstrates (pages 78–79), appears to be that we do no such thing.

Talking about perception and cognition sounds like a pretty rational exercise, but our emotions play a big part in this, too. How we feel (pages 66–67) can influence the kind of information that we absorb and what we can remember What's more, as Aaron T. Beck (pages 68–69) shows, our cognition—what we make of a situation— will play back into our emotions, or how we feel about that situation. This finding has had a profound effect on the treatment of depressive illnesses.

The power of emotion

We also look at emotion itself and where it comes from. A century ago, the belief was that physiological changes in the body (like a surge in adrenaline) triggered our emotions. Now it is seen as being about how we interpret the situation in front of us (pages 72–73), which is in part to do with the society to which we belong. This begs the question of whether emotions, and how we express them, are universal, or specific to certain cultures. Does an emoji in a text message, for example, convey the same meaning anywhere in the world, or are there cultural differences at play (pages 70–71)? This question recurs throughout psychology. Over many decades of the last century, much of psychology was developed at Western universities, with experiments largely carried out on Western students, leading many to ask if this is a broad enough sample from which to develop universal truths about humankind. Emotion also drives how we make decisions (pages 74–75). Pure rationality would get us nowhere, because in every aspect of our lives we could find ourselves processing an infinite amount of information, but sadly lacking the processing speed of a computer. We need an emotional element to help us to rule out a whole bunch of options—helping us to make decisions based on gut feeling so as to be able to get on with our lives. And all this decision making can take a mental and emotional toll on our resources. As Roy Baumeister's experiments appeared to show (pages 76–77), it is possible simply to run out of the capacity to decide. So what would life be like with fewer challenges? Deeply unfulfilling, according to Mihaly Csikszentmihalyi (pages 80–81), whose concept of "flow" is kind of a "sweet spot" in the process of learning; perhaps of our entire life experiences.

BIOGRAPHIES

SIGMUND FREUD (1856–1939)

Freud is widely regarded as a founding father of modern psychology due to his groundbreaking—and at the time, controversial—theories of the human mind. Even though much of his work has been superseded by subsequent research, Freud could be described as an Isaac Newton figure: the fact that many of his findings remain unproven does not detract from their importance. Freud began as a neurologist in private practice in Vienna, specializing in nervous and brain disorders. His work with patients suffering from hysteria led to the foundation of psychoanalysis, and provided the catalyst for subsequent theoretical work that continued for nearly 40 years. Perhaps his greatest legacy was his work on unconscious processes—the idea that we are governed by irrational forces beyond our awareness or control. The broad themes of his work—repression, inner conflicts, defenses against anxiety, dream interpretation, the childhood origins of adult personality, along with how our inner world guides our behavior—have also become staples of psychological research. Even if many of the specifics of Freudian theory no longer form a part of mainstream psychology, his desire to bring a sense of scientific rigor to the study of the mind—and to unhook sexuality from moral judgment—put him ahead of his time.

GEORGE A. MILLER (1920–2012)

Miller studied at Alabama, and gained his Ph.D. at Harvard. He began his research there in the 1940s, looking at speech production and perception, and his *Language and Communication* (1951) helped to establish the new science of psycholinguistics. Building on existing mathematical theories of communication, he published a paper on short-term memory capacity, "The Magical Number Seven, Plus or Minus Two." It captured the public imagination and even encouraged lively debates on the optimal length of telephone numbers. He continued to work on the psychology of speech, testing some of Noam Chomsky's theories, and in 1960 founded (with Jerome Bruner) the Harvard Center for Cognitive Studies. He is regarded (with Chomsky and Bruner) as one of the founding fathers of cognitive psychology, the study of thought processes—a dramatic departure from behavioral psychology, which stated that since mental processes were not observable, they were not suitable for scientific study. After a period at New York's Rockerfeller University, working on language acquisition, Miller moved to Princeton where he helped establish both the Princeton Cognitive Science Laboratory and WordNet, a word database that has applications in present-day search engines and artificial intelligence.

AARON T. BECK (1921–)

Beck is known for his pioneering work in developing cognitive therapy to treat depression and anxiety and, later, a host of other disorders including phobias and even schizophrenia. Educated at Brown University and Yale, where he completed his medical degree, he shifted into psychiatry early on, a field at that time dominated by Freudian psychoanalysis. Beck practiced as a psychoanalyst, but felt that neither this treatment, nor the alternative (medication) offered life-changing solutions. In the 1950s, at the University of Pennsylvania he began to seek empirical evidence for aspects of psychoanalytic thinking relating to depressed patients. He was unsuccessful. Instead, he made a remarkable breakthrough—in discovering that patients' negative beliefs and "automatic thoughts" were driving their mood, he realized that cognitive distortions could be explored, challenged, and ultimately corrected in therapy. He set up the Mood Clinic to test therapeutic approaches under controlled conditions, and began building a detailed technique—cognitive therapy—and a body of evidence for its effectiveness. Since 1992 he has been emeritus professor at the University of Pennsylvania, where he is director of the Aaron T. Beck Psychopathology Research Center.

ELIZABETH LOFTUS (1944–)

Loftus is a world authority on the unreliability of human memory, most famously in relation to eyewitness testimony and courtroom procedure, as well as in the field of false memory and, more recently, aspects of what could be called "mind control." After completing her psychology doctorate at Stanford, Loftus carried out some breakthrough research on eyewitness testimony that revealed how far human memory could be affected by the questions used to prompt recall—even to the point of witnesses planting misinformation, based on what they had (falsely) come to believe they had seen or experienced. The implications for miscarriages of justice were obvious, and Loftus, as an expert witness, took part in dozens of courtroom trials, including the Bosnian war crime hearings in The Hague, and the trial of the Oklahoma bomber in 1997. In the 1990s, she also became involved in work on false memory—both in the lab, where she was able to prove that it is possible to "implant" a false memory, and in the courts, where she investigated (not without controversy) accusations of child abuse that were being made on the basis of "recovered memories"—memories that had surfaced during psychotherapy, which the therapist believed had been repressed.

CAN YOU REMEMBER SEVEN THINGS?

THE MAIN CONCEPT | How is it that I can remember the two-hour route to my sister's house, but struggle to remember a new phone number? This highlights what we could call long-term and short-term memory, a distinction first formulated in 1890 by William James, who observed the "ordinary, lasting memory" versus the "rapid, immediate memory" that seems to allow us to remember things for just as long as required. This model of the mind, with two different kinds of memory stores, endured for nearly a century. In the 1950s, cognitive psychologist George A. Miller wrote a paper called "The Magical Number Seven, Plus or Minus Two," which aimed to show just how much information short-term memory could hold. Not much, in fact. Miller believed there were only between five and nine "slots" in short-term memory to contain information. Beyond that, something must be forgotten to make way for something new. Nonetheless, our capacity can be increased if information is organized into meaningful patterns that are easier to store—which is why phone numbers are "chunked" into groups of digits. Since the 1970s, more sophisticated memory models have emerged—seeing memory as a single store where some items have been stored more profoundly than others. It all depends on the level of meaning or cognition we give something when we come across it.

THE EVIDENCE | Miller's "magic number" came from an extensive review of experimental data, including the results of tests carried out by Irwin Pollack. Pollack had asked listeners to identify musical tones by assigning numbers to each one. With four different tones, confusions were rare, but with five to eight tones, confusion became common. Miller also examined variations on the Pollack tests carried out by other researchers, as well as further work on visual memory and on more complex memory tasks. The more information requiring retention, the cruder and more inaccurate that retention became, whereas with around seven "bits" of information (including "chunked" information), participants across all these studies managed to recall with some accuracy.

THE WIDER PICTURE | *Short-term memory is now more commonly seen as just a part of Alan Baddeley and Graham Hitch's 1974 model of the "working memory," a framework of structures and processes used for the temporary storage and manipulation of information—calling up data from elsewhere in the brain, and holding words/sounds and images on a kind of temporary "scratch pad." And the limitations on how much short-term data we can retain may be even lower than Miller suggested.*

COGNITIVE PSYCHOLOGY
Page 14
GEORGE A. MILLER BIOGRAPHY
Page 56
UNRELIABLE MEMORIES
Page 62

REPRESSION OF MEMORIES

THE MAIN CONCEPT | If you have a particularly unpleasant, frightening, or traumatic experience, is it possible to lock the memory of it away? The idea that highly emotionally charged memories can be repressed became an important part of the work of Sigmund Freud at the start of the twentieth century. He came to believe that the process of repression was an unconscious one, designed to defend ourselves from unbearable thoughts, mental conflicts, or events. The repressed memory was not destroyed, but instead lurked beyond our awareness and control in our unconscious, at times trying to break through to the surface through dreams or misplaced words (the Freudian slip), and more commonly making itself felt through physical symptoms for which there was no apparent physiological cause: the various kinds of neuroses that were to be found among Freud's patients in Vienna around the start of the twentieth century. As an example: a young woman experienced severe and unexplained pains in her legs. She eventually recalled pains she had felt when nursing her sick father, who had rested his heavy legs on her lap while she changed his dressings. She had also felt resentment at having to nurse her father, and subsequently, guilt at her resentment. In Freud's view, the difficult feelings had been repressed— and her physical leg pains were the consequence of this.

PSYCHOANALYSIS
Page 10

ERIKSON'S EIGHT STAGES OF MAN
Page 38

SIGMUND FREUD BIOGRAPHY
Page 56

THE EVIDENCE | Trying to show repression of memory in a lab setting has been difficult. In a 1961 study by George Levinger and James Clark, participants were given a list of negatively charged words like "anger" and "war," as well as neutral words like "window" or "tree," and asked to come up with a word association. When asked later to recall these associations, the participants found the negatively charged words (which had prompted higher stress levels) more difficult to recall than the neutral words. Some, such as Paul Klein, saw this as irrefutable proof of repression. But further studies demonstrated that as time elapsed after the experiment, emotionally charged words were in fact recalled more clearly.

THE WIDER PICTURE | *A century after Freud, the concept of repression has crucial social and legal importance in relation to those people who appear to recover lost memories of abuse, decades later, often during the process of therapy. Psychologists have shown how in some situations, it is possible to provoke false memories (see pages 62–63). We typically feel we own our memories, so consider them reliable. It is a shock to have to question that.*

UNRELIABLE MEMORIES

THE MAIN CONCEPT | How much can you trust your own memories? In the early twentieth century, British psychologist Frederic Bartlett found that memory does not really work like a camera—rather, it is prone to inaccuracies, influences, and interpretations based on prior experiences: our own sets of beliefs, knowledge, and assumptions ("mental schemas"). The kinds of prompts and questions we encounter affect accurate recall, too. Elizabeth Loftus showed that the validity of all memories was questionable (see opposite), including "flashbulb" memories—episodic and highly emotional memories, considered to be highly accurate due to their near-photographic detail. For a flashbulb memory to occur, the event or conditions must be surprising, unexpected, and emotionally and personally significant. A 2003 study by Martin Conway and others in the United States found that the majority of participants had near-perfect memory of the 9/11 attacks on the Twin Towers, when recalled a year later. Such memories, though, are a rare exception, and even apparent flashbulb memories can be unreliable. Cognitive psychologist Ulric Neisser found that when such memories were explored in detail, they often contained false material. For Neisser, it was the repeated discussion of momentous events that created the memories, not, as some had thought, some special brain activity.

THE EVIDENCE | How easily can memories be manipulated? In 1974 Elizabeth Loftus and John Palmer put this to the test in an experiment to observe how language affects the way people recall memories. Students were shown images of a car crash. Some were asked how fast they believed the two vehicles were traveling when they "hit" each other, while for others the question was worded as "smashed into" each other, or "bumped" into or "contacted" each other. The choice of words used had a significant effect: there was a clear difference in students' estimates, with "smashed into" prompting the highest estimates of speed, at 41 miles (65 km) per hour, and "contacted" the lowest, at just 32 miles (50 km) per hour.

THE WIDER PICTURE | *The effect of leading questions, demonstrated in lab experiments, has had an important bearing on the perceived reliability of eyewitness testimony in law courts, because our recollections of events can so easily be swayed by how we are being asked to remember. In fact, our memories can be subject to distortion and change each time they are recalled.*

ELIZABETH LOFTUS BIOGRAPHY
Page 57

BOWLBY & DEPRIVATION
Page 28

WHY FAKE NEWS HITS THE TARGET
Page 82

WHEN YOUR BELIEFS COLLIDE

THE MAIN CONCEPT | When it comes to attitudes and beliefs, do you tend to stick to what you believe, or do you adapt your beliefs in light of new information? Research shows that when our beliefs come into contact with attitudes that conflict with them, we get uneasy and tend to find other ways to justify and adhere to what we believe. If, for instance, you love cats, and you also love your new couch, but your cat really loves to scratch the new couch, you might adapt your thinking about the couch: "It wasn't that great anyway." Or your cat: "Maybe I don't love cats so much after all." The point is that the sense of unease that comes when our attitudes are undermined by contrary evidence—termed "cognitive dissonance" by American psychologist Leon Festinger in 1957—can lead us to adapt new attitudes to restore a sense of harmony: we seek ways to make newfound evidence consistent with our beliefs. In 1956, Festinger, Henry Riecken, and Stanley Schachter studied a religious cult that believed its home city would be destroyed on a precise date, unless cult members sold all their possessions: then they would be rescued by aliens. Neither the apocalypse nor the alien rescue materialized. But cult members, left with no possessions (and plenty of cognitive dissonance) quickly adapted their beliefs, claiming that their actions had prevented the destruction happening in the first place.

THE EVIDENCE | In 1959 Festinger and James Carlsmith invited participants to take part in a "very boring task" (turning pegs in slots for one hour). In return, half the participants received $1, and half got $20. Afterward, they were all asked to lie to another group of people, telling them that the task was very interesting. When interviewed later, those paid $20 still thought the one-hour task had been boring. But those paid $1 saw it in a more positive light. Why? Because they experienced a clash of beliefs: the task was very boring; *and* they had been forced to lie about it; *and* they only got paid a measly $1. This left them with no positive takeaway. So they tweaked their view of the task: "Actually, it was moderately enjoyable."

THE WIDER PICTURE | *We are constantly struggling with cognitive dissonance, whether we are feeling trapped in a relationship and telling ourselves it is okay—or working hard on a disastrous project and telling ourselves the work is easy. Confronting the dissonance head-on means facing difficult truths and thinking about them, something even the most rational of us are loath to do.*

BEING IN SOMEONE ELSE'S SHOES
Page 78
WHY FAKE NEWS HITS THE TARGET
Page 82
GROUPTHINK: WE KNOW BEST
Page 100

HOW FEELINGS BRING ON MEMORIES

THE MAIN CONCEPT | Do you ever lie awake at night worrying? If you do, you might start with one anxious thought and then find that a whole bunch of others start to come into your mind. One idea of why this happens— why this apparent door opens and all the bad stuff flows out—is to do with how our emotional state affects memory. Cognitive psychologist Gordon Bower explored this connection in a series of experiments that led to the conclusions that people tend to pay more attention to, and learn more about, events that match their emotional state (mood congruity). It is also easier to recall an event if people are able to reinstate the mood that they felt when they experienced it ("mood-dependent retrieval"). Fundamentally, events or information and emotion are stored together in memory. Bower speculated that these emotional shortcuts to mood-congruent memories could be responsible for the anxious person finding it easy to associate and recall one anxiety with a host of other worries (and hence a sleepless night); or for someone happy to more easily remember positive events, ramping up a good mood. There are implications here for self-help: if you find something distracting or positive to act as a switch, then you may be able to activate a different mental path, taking you from an angry mood or an anxious state to more positive thoughts.

THE EVIDENCE | One of Bower's experiments involved college students, specifically those who were able to be successfully hypnotized into either a happy or a sad state. They were then asked to memorize lists of words. Later, and again under hypnosis in either a happy or sad state, they were asked to recall the words. The result was that words learned in the sad or happy state were more easily recalled when the participant's mood matched their emotional state when learning. In a further experiment, participants kept a diary of events, and were asked to recall the events under hypnosis. Again, when their emotional state during recall matched the emotions linked with the events, recall was more accurate.

THE WIDER PICTURE | *How we feel will affect the kind of details that we notice—sad people pick up on the sad or negative aspects of a story or a situation, and happy people pull out the positive aspects. Our feelings, according to Bower, are like a magnet that draws iron filings up from a heap of dust—how we feel will affect the kind of information we pick up, as well as the things that we can most easily remember.*

UNRELIABLE MEMORIES
Page 62
PERCEPTIONS THAT DRIVE YOUR MOOD
Page 68
FEAR IS MORE THAN JUST ADRENALINE
Page 72

PERCEPTIONS THAT DRIVE YOUR MOOD

THE MAIN CONCEPT | Which of these two statements about depression seems the most convincing to you: "I am in a low mood; consequently, I feel the world is hopeless and I am worthless," or "I feel the world is hopeless and I am worthless, and consequently I am in a low mood"? If you went with the second statement, then you are aligning yourself with the cognitive theory of depression, developed by Aaron T. Beck in 1967, which holds that depression stems from a persons's set of intensely negative and irrational beliefs, taking them in a downward spiral to depression. If beliefs drive depression, then Beck maintained that an antidote to depression would be to alleviate these distorted or irrational beliefs, and replace them with more positive or rational ones—a kind of "glass-half-full" approach. This cognitive aspect of depression was also explored by psychologist Martin Seligman, who looked at the link between prior experiences of helplessness (perhaps in illness, or a bad childhood experience) and the development of depression. Not everyone who encountered negative prior experiences developed depression, however, and in later research, Seligman, along with Lyn Abramson and John Teasdale, reasoned that it was dependent on the explanations that people used to account for the things that happened to them. Beliefs, then, can be a major factor in how we feel.

THE EVIDENCE | Beck's research was all about gathering evidence, which in part stemmed from his dissatisfaction with traditional Freudian psychoanalsysis (which he used to practice) and which he felt produced very little by way of evidence of its effectiveness. Beck devised his "Depression Inventory", which he used in the 1960s to record mood changes, motivation, and the patient's cognitive approach. This groundbreaking attempt to measure mood and ways of thinking went on to form the basis of his cognitive therapy treatment—known today as CBT—using treatment protocols that could be written into operating manuals, and using standard measurements throughout the treatment. It created a huge body of evidence, and helped ensure the take-up of cognitive therapy across the world.

COGNITIVE PSYCHOLOGY
Page 14
AARON T. BECK BIOGRAPHY
Page 57
SELIGMAN & DEPRESSION
Page 138

THE WIDER PICTURE | *The model of perceptions and beliefs driving depression has proved to be influential, and Cognitive Behavioral Therapy has proved an effective way of dealing with some patients suffering with depression by working on how they perceive the situation they are in. What's more, the relatively short duration of the treatment (as few as eight sessions) has made it popular with health providers.*

THE UNIVERSALITY OF THE EMOJI

THE MAIN CONCEPT | Next time you insert an emoji into a text message, consider this: Does everyone in the world use facial expressions to convey their emotions in exactly the same way? Are emotions, and how we express them, truly universal? In 1872, Charles Darwin identified the expression of a core group of emotions (such as fear and anger) that he believed we are all born with: innate patterns of behavior that are a part of our evolutionary development. A century later, researchers began to explore the idea of universal emotions afresh. In 1966, Charles Osgood identified seven main groups of facial expressions signaling emotion that seemed to be common to all of humanity (surprise, fear, happiness, sadness, anger, interest, and disgust). Around the same time, Paul Ekman started a global project on facial expressions and emotions (see opposite), exploring how universal these expressions are. Since then, there has been a good deal of additional research, including new sets of facial images across many ethnicities, and some of the findings run counter to Ekman's ideas of "universality." In 2012 Rachael Jack and others found evidence to suggest that rather than being exclusively hardwired into our nature, many of the facial expressions we use to express emotion are molded by our social environment—a "nurture" aspect—which may explain some of the differences that occur.

THE EVIDENCE | Ekman traveled the globe to gather evidence of facial expressions, inviting participants to look at photos of people's faces expressing various emotions, and then to identify which emotions they believed were being expressed. His work extended from remote tribes in Papua New Guinea through to North and South America and Japan, and revealed that nearly all of us understand the same facial expressions in exactly the same way. Later, Ekman (with Wallace Friesen) used detailed photography and filming to identify exactly which muscles are used in the expressions we make, creating a sophisticated database of facial expressions known as Facial Action Coding System (FACS)—now a key tool in many areas of mental health research.

THE WIDER PICTURE | *The vast database of facial expressions that is FACS has provided scope for further research into how different people are able to "read" facial expressions. These include teenagers—who, despite their expertise in using emojis, can struggle with the real thing—and people who suffer from psychotic illnesses that render them almost completely incapable of reading facial expressions.*

FEAR IS MORE THAN JUST ADRENALINE
Page 72

WORK IN PROGRESS
Page 128

NORMALITY: WHO'S THE JUDGE?
Page 136

FEAR IS MORE THAN JUST ADRENALINE

THE MAIN CONCEPT | Cognitive researchers into depression (see Aaron T. Beck, pages 68–69) believe that our emotions (feeling low, for example) can stem from the attitudes and beliefs we hold. This kind of thinking is part of a long line of research into where our emotions come from. Back in the late nineteenth century the thinking on this was completely different. Introspective psychologists (notably William James and, independently, Carl Lange) proposed that first we feel a physical response to an event (a quickening heartbeat, a rush of adrenaline) and only then, as a result of that, do we feel the emotion. We don't weep because we feel sad, James suggested: we feel sad because we weep. This approach—dubbed the James–Lange theory—prompted researchers (such as Albert Ax) to explore whether different emotions were linked with different physiological changes in the body. He found that they were. But in the 1920s, Walter Cannon (who discovered the "fight or flight" response) argued that physiological changes like sweating, or a faster heartbeat, had nothing at all to do with the emotional response, which is based purely on how we make sense of what's going on: the meaning we attribute to our experience. This became the prevailing view, and this cognitive aspect was explored in a series of experiments by Stanley Schachter and Jerome Singer in the 1960s (see opposite).

THE EVIDENCE | Schachter and Singer injected a number of participants with adrenaline, and then put them into two different environments. One was designed to induce a sense of euphoria, thanks to a planted actor participant joking about with paper airplanes and creating a sense of fun; the other was intended to induce a sense of anger, with another actor having a tantrum and creating a stressful scene. The results showed that while participants would have been experiencing the physical effects induced by the adrenaline (sweating, faster heartbeat) that are usually linked with fear or anger, their actual emotional response was almost entirely influenced by the mood (fun or fury) set by the actors.

THE WIDER PICTURE | *If a bad thing happens and it is someone else's fault, we may feel anger. If, however, it is our fault, we may feel shame. Or we may not. The shame response depends on the social environment in which we grew up. So while cognitive aspects are part and parcel of how we experience emotions, our cognitions themselves (and hence our emotions) depend on social aspects, too.*

KOHLBERG & MORALITY
Page 42

HOW FEELINGS BRING ON MEMORIES
Page 66

THE UNIVERSALITY OF THE EMOJI
Page 70

WHY COLD LOGIC NEEDS HOT EMOTION

THE MAIN CONCEPT | Do you decide with your head or with your heart? The belief that making a good decision involves cold, unemotional reason is widespread. But in reality, we make our best and perhaps fastest decisions when head and heart—or logic and emotions—work in tandem. This idea sprang from work by Antonio Damasio, an American neurologist who studied brain-damaged patients. He observed that damage to the prefrontal cortex (where the brain connects emotions with reasoning), appeared to shut off the physical response to emotional stimuli. Showing patients images designed to shock or excite, for example, did not provoke the expected changes in heart rate or electrodermal activity (shifts in the skin's electrical conductivity). But at the same time, such damage also appeared to destroy any powers of decision-making: one patient would deliberate endlessly over simple decisions such as which color pen to use to sign a form, or when to schedule the next meeting. Investigating further, Damasio and colleagues found that decisions made purely on reason are not only more difficult, but they can also be worse than decisions where emotion is present. This, they found, can even apply to card games, where a certain measure of anxiety can help players make better decisions.

THE UNIVERSALITY OF THE EMOJI
Page 70

CAN YOU RUN OUT OF WILLPOWER?
Page 76

WHERE IS IT KEPT?
Page 122

THE EVIDENCE | The most famous of Damasio's cases is that of Elliot, a businessman whose life fell apart following surgery for a brain tumor. His intellect, memory, and social skills appeared to be intact, but he made a series of very bad decisions, losing his job, going bankrupt, losing his wife— and his second wife. Damasio began to realize that Elliot never displayed emotion, and further testing of this (using flashcards of scenes that would normally arouse emotions, such as gruesome accidents or sex scenes) had zero effect on Elliot. Looking at evidence from fifty cases of patients with similar incidents of brain damage, Damasio came to see that emotion was a crucial part of effective decision-making.

THE WIDER PICTURE | *Damasio's discoveries led to his "somatic marker hypothesis"—the idea that we accumulate physical (somatic) feelings or "markers" about putting ourselves in any given situation. These markers, which can give us a good or a bad feeling, help us to rule out dozens of options that would otherwise overwhelm us and make decision-making impossible. Or as people often say: "I can't decide. I'll go with my gut feeling."*

CAN YOU RUN OUT OF WILLPOWER?

THE MAIN CONCEPT | As President, Barack Obama famously admitted (to *Vanity Fair*) that he wore only gray or blue suits so that he could pare down the number of decisions he made in a day. He seemed to be implying that making too many decisions can erode your ability to make yet more (or effective) decisions as the day wears on—what could be called "decision fatigue." The idea comes from research in 1996 by Roy Baumeister, who coined the phrase "ego depletion." His experimental work (see opposite) was taken to imply that we have finite resources of willpower, and that struggling to exert self-control over one task can have a detrimental effect on our ability to complete subsequent tasks. Willpower could also be depleted by making decisions or tackling a difficult task. Baumeister's ideas led to a mass of research in subsequent decades, and a huge body of literature (more than eighty published papers) built up on ego depletion that seemed, according to Martin Hagger in 2010, to confirm the theory's validity. It also prompted a boom in self-help literature and popular theories, with the idea that we may be most effective in the morning (with the willpower stock at its peak) and that procrastination in the afternoon is the result of ego depletion earlier in the day.

THE EVIDENCE | Baumeister's original theory was based on four separate experiments, the most famous of which involved chocolate cookies. Each participant was left alone in a room with a plate of warm chocolate cookies straight from the oven, and a plate of radishes. Participants were told to eat only the food assigned to them, either cookies, or radishes. Straight afterward, all were given the task of solving difficult puzzles (they were, in fact, impossible to solve). Participants who had eaten only the radishes gave up on the puzzle much faster than those who had eaten the cookies, suggesting that exercising self-restraint earlier (that is, not stealing a few cookies) had taken its toll on their willingness to work on the next task.

THE WIDER PICTURE | *Whether exercising self-control, making decisions, or concentrating on a task, our will to continue seems to get worn down, like tired muscles. The solution? Low blood sugar levels could be a cause—brain work, after all, consumes fuel, so we must eat. Engaging in strictly controlled activities such as a fitness regime has also been shown to boost willpower: you can work the body and the mind at the same time.*

WHY COLD LOGIC NEEDS HOT EMOTION
Page 74

HOW TO BE IN THE ZONE
Page 80

WE'RE NOT ALWAYS LIKE THIS
Page 126

BEING IN SOMEONE ELSE'S SHOES

THE MAIN CONCEPT | All of us—whether we are fans of psychology or not—spend a lot of time trying to work out why people do what they do. "Why did that car nearly run me down on the crossing this evening? Is the driver a psychopath?" This kind of thinking, where we start to attribute personality characteristics to people on the basis of their actions, happens all the time. How far we are prepared to be judgmental or understanding of what other people are doing depends on various factors, including whether the act appears to be deliberate or accidental, or whether it appears to have been aimed specifically at you, or whether you just "got in the way." One key aspect of this kind of theorizing is so pervasive that social psychologist Lee Ross called it "fundamental attribution error," and it concerns every one of us. If you almost hit a pedestrian while driving, you might say: "I didn't see him because it was dark. He was wearing really dark clothing." But if you saw someone else almost hit a pedestrian, you would say: "He must be a maniac to drive like that." So we tend to think that our behavior is shaped by our circumstances, whereas we see everybody else's as shaped by the kind of person they are.

THE EVIDENCE | One of the earliest studies into fundamental attribution error comes from the 1970s (evidently a more heteronormative era): Richard Nisbett and colleagues asked a group of male students to write down why they had chosen to study their particular subject and, also, why they liked their girlfriends. They were then asked to write down why a close friend had chosen the course, and why this man had chosen his own girlfriend. The results showed that when talking about themselves, they framed their answers in terms of specific attributes about the course ("it's interesting"), or about their girlfriends ("she's smart"). In comparison, when writing about their friends, the results focused on the kind of person they thought their friend was ("he's into math"; "he likes dancers").

THE WIDER PICTURE | *Making excuses for bad driving, or questioning a bunch of hairy 1970s students about their girlfriends may sound a little remote, but this bias in our thinking affects real lives. A person receiving welfare may be seen by many to be a lazy scrounger, whereas if you or I were on welfare, we might explain that we'd simply been unable to find a job. Putting ourselves in someone else's shoes changes everything.*

WHY FAKE NEWS HITS THE TARGET
Page 82

IT'S ALWAYS US & THEM
Page 104

THE BEAUTY BIAS
Page 112

HOW TO BE
IN THE ZONE

THE MAIN CONCEPT | Video game designers know that the secret of getting someone hooked on a game is to provide just the right balance of challenge and skill. Too much challenge and you get stressed and frustrated. But when you have all the skills and not enough challenge, the game gets boring. The perfect combination of the two, between boredom and excitement, where you "lose yourself" in the activity, confronting the challenges of striving for a chosen goal while putting your skills into practice, is a highly satisfying place to be. And not just in gaming. It exists in all activities of life, from elite sports to baking a cake, and from all kinds of creative pursuits through to doodling on the side of a page. In the 1970s the Hungarian psychologist Mihaly Csikszentmihalyi coined the term "flow" to describe this state, and the concept has gained traction since then as part of the positive psychology movement—a strand of research aimed at defining well-being and finding ways of achieving it. A few decades earlier, Abraham Maslow was writing about a "hierarchy of needs": after the essential basics of food, water, and security, we also seek safety, love, and esteem, while at the pinnacle is "self-actualization," realizing ourselves to the fullest. Flow theory is a kind of shortcut to the top.

THE EVIDENCE | Observing flow in actions requires methods of "experience sampling," asking participants to record their responses during activities (there is, of course, a risk that interrupting the flow like this can destroy it). In his "Beeper Study," Csikszentmihalyi gave a group of teenagers each a beeper that went off at random intervals, at which point they were asked to record what they were doing and how they were feeling. Most of the time they were not particularly happy, with the exception of when they were fully engaged on a challenging task, a result that seemed to back up the flow state conditions for enjoyment. More recent research has centered on what makes up so-called "autotelic" personalities—people who seem prone to seek out and enjoy flow-like activities.

THE WIDER PICTURE | *Is flow available to everyone? It can depend on upbringing, schooling, or the stage of life we are in. Many teens actually hate flow activities, seeking low-challenge relaxation as an antidote to the stress of schoolwork. The challenge, to schools and to workplaces, is to find ways to bring flow principles into busy, multitasking daily life.*

HUMANISTIC PSYCHOLOGY
Page 16
MASLOW'S HIERARCHY OF NEEDS
Page 106
HARD GRAFT OR GENIUS?
Page 132

WHY FAKE NEWS HITS THE TARGET

THE MAIN CONCEPT | Part of the appeal—as well as the danger and potency—of "fake news" seems to be that it is targeted at people who already want to believe it. It feeds into their existing frame of beliefs. Information that might run counter to these views is discounted—and is itself dismissed as fake news. However, the tendency to give weight to information and arguments that support our beliefs rather than upend them is something we are all prone to do, and is known as "confirmation bias." The process of inductive reasoning—where we try to draw conclusions based on evidence—can be wildly inaccurate if we lack sufficient information. So we take shortcuts, based on the evidence to hand, or taking just one example and making that representative of everything: "We had a colder than average winter, so global warming is a hoax." Confirmation bias kicks in when we seek only information that supports our existing view, and we discount unhelpful evidence, for example, the body of scientific evidence that challenges that view. A Pew Research Center survey in 2016 found that among a sample of scientifically knowledgeable US voters, 23 percent of Republican supporters believed that human activity was causing global warming, compared with 93 percent of Democrat party supporters. Confirmation bias was most likely at work on both sides of the political divide.

WHEN YOUR BELIEFS COLLIDE
Page 64

BEING IN SOMEONE ELSE'S SHOES
Page 78

GROUPTHINK: WE KNOW BEST
Page 100

THE EVIDENCE | In a study by Geoffrey Munro, a group of students were asked whether they believed homosexuality was linked with mental illness. The group was then divided in two. Half were shown research that supported a link between mental illness and homosexuality (the papers were faked, but looked real). The other half were shown research with the opposite view. The students were then asked if the homosexuality/mental illness question was one that could be answered by scientific research. Those who had had their views supported by the research agreed that it could. However, those who had had their views challenged thought science had nothing to offer on the subject—nor on a wide range of other topics they were asked about. Science was rubbishing their view of the world, so they rubbished science.

THE WIDER PICTURE | *Confirmation bias has been found to work even more powerfully in groups than it does with individuals. In 2000, Stefan Schulz-Hardt and his colleagues showed that the more like-minded the group, and the less dissent is expressed, the more biased its members will be in searching for information to support their ideas. The implications for social media users are all too clear.*

"The line between good and evil is permeable and almost anyone can be induced to cross it when pressured by situational forces."

PHILIP ZIMBARDO,
IN AN INTERVIEW WITH HANS SHERRER (2003)

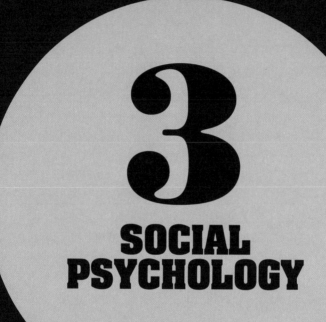

3
SOCIAL
PSYCHOLOGY

INTRODUCTION

This chapter is about how we as individuals are affected by, and work with—or against—the people around us. Undoubtedly our behaviors and beliefs are influenced by others. Solomon Asch showed that peer pressure is enough to make some of us deny the facts in front of our very eyes (pages 90–91). Conversely, Serge Moscovici took up the subject a decade later with work on how minority viewpoints can provoke a challenge to entrenched beliefs and spark change (pages 92–93). Meanwhile, in situations where dissent is absent, ignored, dismissed, or neutralized within a group, we can end up with what Irving Janis termed "groupthink" (pages 100–101) to explain a collection of catastrophic foreign-policy decisions in the United States in the 1960s.

The power of groups

Social psychology took off in the postwar years, and the memory of the Holocaust was a backdrop to much research on humankind's capacity for causing suffering and harm, prompting some of the most famous experiments in psychology. In the early 1960s, Stanley Milgram (pages 94–95) conducted his obedience experiments involving the use of "electric shocks," research that in turn led to decades of further study and debate about how and why we are willing to obey authority. In the 1970s, Philip Zimbardo created the Stanford "Prison" Experiment (pages 96–97), which showed in graphic detail how ordinary students could carry out acts of extraordinary cruelty—not through being extraordinarily cruel people, but simply because of the nature of the environment and role that they found themselves in.

In social situations, we usually find ourselves in some kind of group, whether or not by choice. Groups affect our behavior in myriad ways. If you find yourself in a group that is stigmatized in some way that is directly relevant to what you are trying to achieve, then you can end up underachieving. This phenomenon was dubbed "stereotype threat" by Claude Steele (pages 102–103), and has been used to explore almost every facet of difference and stigma within our society, making it one of the most intensively researched areas of modern psychology.

Group membership influences people in a powerful way. Henri Tajfel (pages 104–105) showed that simply being categorized into a group is enough for people to feel a loyalty and kinship with fellow group members, instantly triggering a sense of "us" and "them." The more unfavorably we are able to view rival groups, he believed, the greater boost of self-esteem we appear to experience. The roots of intergroup conflict, then, don't really need to be about anything much: Tajfel's "social identity theory" suggests that once people are categorized, intergroup differences start to escalate. There is an element of "mob mentality"—though the mob itself exhibits some fascinating traits that have been termed "deindividuation" (pages 110–11)—meaning we cast aside our individual personality and take on that of the group, typically one of disinhibition, extreme arguments, and uncontrolled behavior. This is as true of a fist-waving physical mob as it is of the invisible mob that inhabits social media.

From loafing to loving

Within the widest possible group—the broader society within which we exist—the discipline of positive psychology has explored what it might mean to lead a fulfilled life. One of the earliest theories in this area is that of Abraham Maslow (pages 106–107) whose "hierarchy of needs" shows how mankind will keep striving to satisfy immediate needs and then move on to a higher goal. But what is the highest goal of all and what does it mean to realize one's full potential?

Realizing full potential does not have to be an individual effort, and most of us spend much of our time working on projects and activities with others—at school, at work, or at home. Unlike, say, a colony of ants, each of which appears to be working at 100 percent capacity whenever you set eyes on them, human beings almost always tend to slacken off when working on a group project. This tendency, called "social loafing" (pages 108–109), can be found in almost any group activity that psychologists have managed to test. Groups also inhibit our capacity to act in an emergency. The "bystander effect" (pages 98–99) explores how our awareness of others around us tends to stop us from intervening to help—even in critical situations.

We conclude this chapter with two topics to do with attraction, and ultimately, with falling in love. The idea of attractiveness is closely bound up with an innate sense of "good" (pages 112–13), so we tend to think that attractive people are good on all kinds of other measures. This bias toward beauty starts among preschoolers, and is continually being reinforced (think of any classic fairy tale). The flipside is a bias against the less beautiful. Perhaps a way to get through this—or indeed to break through any inherent bias against any group—is to really get to know people properly. Our final topic introduces Arthur Aron's "36 Questions" (pages 114–15), which get two participants to get to know each other. The questions have been used to help break down prejudice and tension among opposing social groups. And they have even led to participants actually falling in love for real.

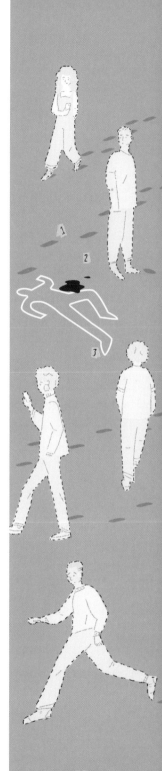

BIOGRAPHIES

SOLOMON ASCH (1907–1996)

Asch was a pioneering social psychologist who made important theoretical contributions to the study of perception, learning, memory, social psychology, and personality theory, but is best known for his experiments on "conformity"—how peer pressure can influence behavior. Born in Warsaw, he moved with his family to the US in 1920, arriving in New York painfully shy and speaking no English. He learned the language fast—by reading Dickens—and proved to be a gifted student, going on to study psychology and taking a master's and Ph.D. at Columbia University. Asch became acquainted with Gestalt psychologists—including Max Wertheimer and Wolfgang Köhler—and shared their desire to take psychology beyond the behaviorist domains of habit formation and response to stimuli, and toward a new kind of study of perception and thinking, leading eventually to the rise of cognitive psychology. In *Social Psychology* (1952) he wrote that his aim was to portray humans as whole beings, rather than as a collection of mechanisms. Asch taught at Swarthmore (the intellectual center for Gestalt in the United States) for 19 years. He left in 1966 to set up the Institute for Cognitive Studies at Rutgers University, finishing his career as emeritus professor at the University of Pennsylvania.

CLAUDE STEELE (1946–)

Steele is best known for his work on "stereotype threat"—broadly, how social stigma can affect the performance of people within the stigmatized group. Born in Chicago in 1946, Steele was raised at the height of the civil rights movement, in which both his parents were actively engaged. In his 2010 book *Whistling Vivaldi*, he recounts how he suddenly became aware of the impact of being black in 1950s America—when he realized he and his friends could not use the local "whites only" swimming pool. Steele graduated with a Ph.D. in social psychology from Ohio State University in 1971, and his early work challenged Leon Festinger's famous "cognitive dissonance" theory with an alternative social psychological explanation—proposing "self-image" as the reason people struggle to retain conflicting beliefs. However, his work on stereotype threat made the biggest impact—showing experimentally how people can underperform when they feel subject to a negative stereotype that has a bearing on what they are trying to achieve. Nor was this exclusively about minority ethnic groups. As Steele writes: "There exists no group on earth that is not negatively stereotyped in some way."

HENRI TAJFEL (1919–1982)

Tajfel is seen as the founding father of a distinctly European social psychology—one that widened the "social" aspect to embrace politics and broader society and culture. He was born in Poland to a middle-class Jewish family, and studied in Paris at the Sorbonne until the outbreak of war in 1939, when he volunteered for the French Army. Captured by the Germans in 1940 (who did not realize he was Jewish), he returned to France after the war to discover that his immediate family had all perished in the Holocaust. He set to work helping orphaned children in France and Belgium, then spent two years working with displaced persons in Germany. In 1951 he moved to London, where he completed a degree in psychology, followed by posts at Oxford, then Bristol. His focus turned to stereotyping and prejudice, and the 1969 paper "Cognitive Aspects of Prejudice" led to later work exploring intergroup prejudice. His experimental work included studies showing how simply categorizing people into groups was enough to make them discriminate in favor of their own group by awarding more money to its members than to members of another group. The inference was that the most "ordinary" people, in an extreme social situation, could develop the kind of prejudice that had destroyed his own family.

STANLEY MILGRAM (1933–1984)

Milgram is famous for his 19 groundbreaking experiments on obedience, carried out at Yale University when he was just 28, and which helped to put the discipline of social psychology into the public consciousness. Milgram was born in the Bronx, to Jewish immigrants from Eastern Europe. An exceptionally gifted student, his first degree was in political science, but he was determined to study psychology at Harvard and after an initial rejection, he undertook a series of summer courses to satisfy the admission requirements—with encouragement from the program director (and pioneering social psychologist), Gordon Allport, who remained a lifelong mentor and friend. At Harvard, Milgram spent time as a research assistant to Solomon Asch, and completed a Ph.D. in social psychology before going to teach at Yale, where his obedience experiments took place. These brought Milgram both celebrity and controversy, with the latter perhaps contributing to the fact that he was not offered a permanent teaching position at Harvard in the following years. He instead moved to City University in New York in 1966, where he remained as professor of psychology until his death at just 51 from a heart attack.

CRUSHING MAJORITIES

THE MAIN CONCEPT | We can all imagine that social interactions might influence how we behave, or what we believe. But how about society influencing our grip on reality itself? Experiments in the 1930s had shown that people's opinions could be easily influenced in situations of uncertainty. But in the 1950s, a set of ingenious experiments (see opposite) by psychologist Solomon Asch at Swarthmore College in Pennsylvania showed that—in lab conditions—peer pressure could even get us to deny hard evidence right in front of our eyes: compelled by a need to conform, people would dismiss factual evidence. Asch's conformity studies are perhaps the most widely replicated experiments of all time, and provided a springboard for decades of further research, revealing nuances of difference according to how well we know the group around us, whether there are other dissenting voices, the level of uncertainty over the evidence, size of groups, and so on. In fact Asch was as interested in measuring levels of independent thinking as he was in examining conformity, and he discovered that with just one person in the group agreeing with a participant's view (i.e., going against the group's erroneous view), the participant would more likely take an independent stand. Asch described himself as an optimist: the pressure to conform is strong, but we still tend to do the right thing.

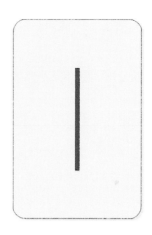

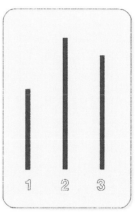

THE EVIDENCE | The most famous conformity experiment had participants shown successive pairs of cards: one card displayed a single line, and the other showed three lines (1, 2, and 3) of varying lengths. Group members had to call out which of the three lines matched the length of the single line. However, only one group member was a genuine participant, unaware that all the others in the group were actors colluding, midway through the experiment, to call out the same wrong answer one after another. Some participants stuck to their guns and contradicted the group to give the right answer. But 32 percent of the participants, many reporting later to have felt extremely conflicted, defied what their eyes were showing them and gave the wrong answer in order to conform to the group.

SOLOMON ASCH BIOGRAPHY
Page 88
HOW ACTIVISTS PREVAIL
Page 92
GROUPTHINK: WE KNOW BEST
Page 100

THE WIDER PICTURE | *Experiments like Asch's line-judgment studies suggest we have a tendency to blind conformity, but there are other interpretations, too. Around 25 percent of the subjects never conformed to group pressure, and even among the conformists, many agonized over the decision. Asch was also interested in the value of dissent—the way that one individual's difference of opinion with a group can prompt discussion and new lines of thinking.*

HOW ACTIVISTS PREVAIL

THE MAIN CONCEPT | In the 1957 film *Twelve Angry Men*, a single, determined, and unnamed jury member—known simply as "Juror 8"—mounts a solo challenge to overturn the "guilty" verdicts of every one of the 11 other jurors. For a lone voice in a large group, there can be enormous pressure to bend to the will of the majority. But sometimes the complete opposite can occur: a strong and resolute minority can start to use its own ideas to change the prevailing attitudes—the abolitionist campaign to end the slave trade is a prime example. Psychologist Serge Moscovici became fascinated with this phenomenon. Coming from a persecuted Jewish minority in Romania, he settled in Paris and later in New York, mixing his own political activism with psychological research into what became known as "minority influence theory," showing how minorities promoting a consistent message can start to bring about attitude change. His findings suggested that we are affected by minorities and majorities in very different ways. Majority views tend to be followed rather passively. Minority views, on the other hand—if strongly held, consistently expressed, and plausible (even if we don't agree with them at first)—can provoke us to challenge entrenched beliefs and possibly even to change our minds.

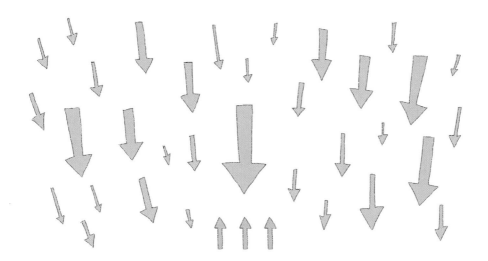

THE EVIDENCE | In a 1969 study by Moscovici and colleagues, 128 female students were divided into groups of six participants, and asked to judge the colors of a series of slides, which displayed the same blue each time, but at different levels of brightness. In each group were four genuine participants plus two actors briefed to claim they were seeing green, not blue. In experiments where the actors claimed to see green for every (blue) slide, a marked influence was observed on other group members, with nearly 9 percent "green" responses coming from the genuine participants across all groups. When the actors claimed to see green on an inconsistent basis, only 1.25 percent of the participants' responses followed suit, suggesting that a very consistent minority view is a key to influencing others.

THE WIDER PICTURE | *To get the best out of a group, minority viewpoints need to be heard. When the majority prevails, thinking becomes convergent and narrow. But when minority viewpoints are heard, assertively and consistently, it forces people to reconsider. In 1986, carrying out further research, Charlan Nemeth found that being exposed to minority points of view helped people to think with more originality—and to find new solutions.*

CRUSHING MAJORITIES
Page 90

THE BYSTANDER EFFECT
Page 98

GROUPTHINK: WE KNOW BEST
Page 100

SHOCKING RESULTS

THE MAIN CONCEPT | Would you commit acts of cruelty, just because you were told to do so by someone in a position of authority? While most of us think we wouldn't, research suggests, alarmingly, that we might. Psychologist Stanley Milgram, mindful of the fate of fellow Jews in the Holocaust, set out to see if ordinary people, against their better judgment, would obey demands from an authority figure simply because they were told to do so. His series of experiments in the early 1960s obliged participants to administer punitive "electric shocks" on other participants, which many of them, amazingly, agreed to do. As well as an instant ethical outcry over the methodology, the results prompted decades of further research and heated debate about how far situational factors could override someone's personality traits. It is far from clear-cut, though. The situational setup appears to matter, but when changes are made, results can be hard to predict. And personality traits and beliefs have also been shown to play a key part; behavior depends on how much participants identify, respect, believe in, or sympathize with the person giving the orders—or, conversely, with the victim. It depends, in other words, on which way their moral compass is already pointing. This is more complex (and more reassuring) than claiming that any of us can be persuaded to blindly obey orders to carry out cruel acts.

THE EVIDENCE | Milgram invited 40 participants to take part in what he told them was a "learning and punishment study." An authoritative-looking "scientist" figure in a lab coat instructed participants to test the learning skills of a second participant located in an adjacent room. They were instructed to punish incorrect answers to a set of questions by administering electric shocks of increasing intensity—prompting excruciating cries of pain and distress. The result was that 65 percent of participants were willing to deliver electric shocks up to the maximum 450 volts when asked to do so. In fact, neither the electric shocks nor the cries of pain were real (the second participant was an actor)—but the men in the study administering the shocks did not know this.

THE WIDER PICTURE | *Many of Milgram's participants showed real anxiety about what they were being asked to do, and the controversy provoked by this study, as well as by Philip Zimbardo's "prison" experiment (pages 96–97), proved to be an ethical watershed. Social psychology research began to adopt ethical rules of what could and could not be done to participants in the name of research.*

STANLEY MILGRAM BIOGRAPHY
Page 89
CRUSHING MAJORITIES
Page 90
EVIL IN THE BEST OF US
Page 96

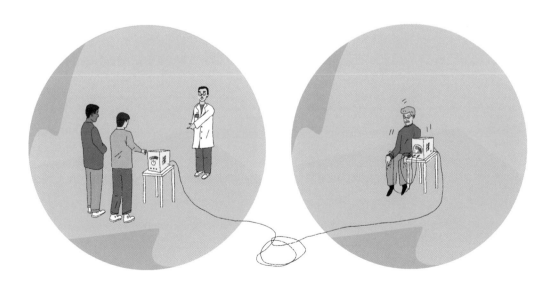

EVIL IN THE BEST OF US

THE MAIN CONCEPT | What makes "ordinary" people carry out monstrous acts? In August 1971, Stanford psychologist Philip Zimbardo carried out what has become one of the most famous social psychology experiments of all time (see opposite), showing that, when put into a certain social role (in this case, jailer or prisoner), college students were capable of committing acts of extraordinary cruelty. So cruel, in fact, that the experiment had to be abandoned. Zimbardo's aim was to shed light on abusive behavior in prisons. The key factor, he demonstrated, was not individual personalities or dispositions, but was more closely linked with the social roles that are created and taken up, the situations that arise, and the expectations of how someone in a particular role should behave. As Zimbardo chillingly surmised: "Any deed that any human being has ever done, however horrible, is possible for any of us to do—under the right or wrong situational pressures." One part of these situational pressures is the formation of groups and the inherent rivalry this creates. Ten years before the prison experiment, Muzafer and Carolyn Sherif had brought together two close-knit teams of 11-year-old boys and set them up in competition (the so-called "Robber's Cave" experiment). The result was prejudice, name-calling, and bitter rivalry. Happily, the boys all made friends again afterward.

THE EVIDENCE | Zimbardo's team recruited student participants, all of whom had passed psychological assessments, and arbitrarily divided them into a group of nine guards, and nine prisoners. The experiment began with the prisoners being arrested, handcuffed, and booked by police in a disorientating and humiliating process. They were put into prison garb and incarcerated in makeshift cells in a university basement (which the experimenters monitored with hidden cameras and bugs). The guards were left to create their own rules for running the prison, but after facing a prisoner mutiny on Day 2, they became harsh and abusive, and a pathological cycle of aggression, sadistic punishment, and psychological abuse took hold that brought some prisoner participants close to breakdown. The experiment was abandoned six days into the two-week program.

THE WIDER PICTURE | *What drives ordinary people to commit monstrous acts is, sadly, a recurrent question in our collective history, whether we consider the events of the Holocaust, Stalinist Russia, the Bosnian war crimes, or the abuses in the Abu Ghraib jail in Iraq. Zimbardo's study was groundbreaking as it demonstrated that if social or institutional situations can create evil acts, institutional change can help prevent it.*

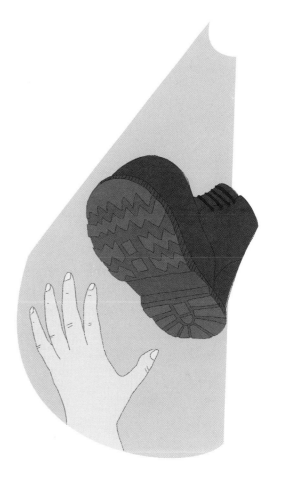

SHOCKING RESULTS
Page 94

IT'S ALWAYS US & THEM
Page 104

LOST IN THE CROWD
Page 110

THE BYSTANDER EFFECT

THE MAIN CONCEPT | In the early hours of Friday March 13, 1964, 28-year-old bar manager Catherine "Kitty" Genovese was attacked by Winston Moseley and stabbed to death outside her apartment in New York City. The event caused a moral outcry and media furore because it was reported that 38 people witnessed her murder, but not a single person did anything to help. (In later years, that figure was disputed; it is likely to have been fewer than ten). The story prompted social psychologists John Darley and Bibb Latané to conduct research (see opposite) into what came to be known as the "bystander effect." This occurs when the presence of others makes it less likely for an individual to offer help to a victim or intervene in an emergency situation than if they had been acting alone. Several things can contribute to this, including confusion and ambiguity over what is actually being witnessed; diffusion of responsibility (we think "someone else will help," and so therefore give up responsibility in doing anything ourselves); and social influence (we look to others to determine how we should act). Winston Moseley, convicted of the murder, appeared to have been already well aware of the bystander effect. When asked how he dared to kill a woman in front of so many witnesses, he simply replied, "I knew they wouldn't do anything, people never do."

THE WIDER PICTURE | *The bystander effect is often characterized as having everyone witness the same thing, with responsibility to act being diffused through the group. In 2016, Kyle Thomas and colleagues showed how there could be much more subtle factors at play: for example, if an individual thinks that others present are aware that the individual knows help is needed. In other words, do others know that that individual is turning a blind eye?*

THE EVIDENCE | Darley and Latané's "smoke-filled room" studies in 1968 were designed to explore how individuals reacted to an emergency situation, either on their own or in the presence of others. In one test, a single participant was left to fill out a questionnaire in a room to which the experimenters began to add smoke; 75 percent of participants left promptly to report the smoke. In a second test, there were three participants in the room, and this time just 38 percent of the groups left to get help. In a third test, there was one genuine participant and two actors, or "confederates," who commented on the smoke but did nothing about it. In this instance, only 10 percent of the participants reported the smoke.

CRUSHING MAJORITIES
Page 90

EVIL IN THE BEST OF US
Page 96

LOST IN THE CROWD
Page 110

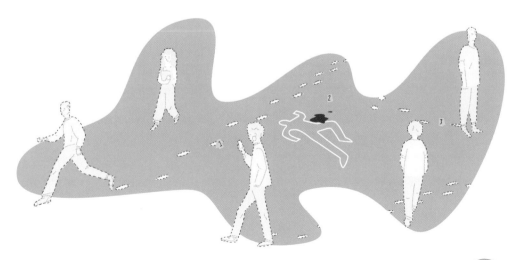

GROUPTHINK: WE KNOW BEST

THE MAIN CONCEPT | When it comes to foreign policy, a single bad decision can cost hundreds of thousands of lives. So it can be reassuring to know that these critical affairs of state are being handled by a resolute leader and a cohesive team of experienced advisors. Or are they? In the 1970s, psychologist Irving Janis identified that the combination of a tight-knit, like-minded team with a powerful leader, faced with a significant external threat and limited options, leads to a phenomenon he called "groupthink." It generally does not end well. The group puts agreement and certainty ahead of all else—disregarding competing options, and shunning frank discussion. In fact, in its moral certainty and closed-mindedness, dissenting views are silenced, outsiders are stereotyped (for example, as disloyal), private doubts are silenced, and awkward facts are rubbished or kept from the leader's attention. The result is that only a narrow range of options is considered and limited information is examined, leading to a high chance of a bad outcome. Janis drew up his groupthink framework after studying detailed accounts of historical events, including American foreign policy disasters (see opposite). In 1991, Gregory Moorhead, Richard Ference, and Chris Neck identified groupthink conditions operating in the decisions leading to the launch of the *Challenger* space shuttle, which exploded shortly after takeoff with the loss of seven lives.

WHEN YOUR BELIEFS COLLIDE
Page 64

WHY FAKE NEWS HITS THE TARGET
Page 82

HOW ACTIVISTS PREVAIL
Page 92

THE EVIDENCE | How was it that smart, intelligent people like John F. Kennedy and his inner circle could agree to what on paper looked like a hopelessly risky plan? In his 1972 book *Victims of Groupthink*, Irving Janis took a forensic look at the decision-making behind the 1961 American Bay of Pigs operation. Following Fidel Castro's rise to power in Cuba, President Kennedy authorized the CIA's plan for an invasion of Cuba by around 14,000 Cuban exiles who landed at the Bay of Pigs. They were quickly surrounded by 20,000 Cuban troops, who killed many and ransomed the remaining forces. Janis also examined other foreign-policy failures, including Pearl Harbor, Truman's invasion of North Korea, and Johnson's escalation of the Vietnam War. He reported that all of these cases displayed the same dysfunctional pattern of detrimental group processes.

THE WIDER PICTURE | *Plenty of bad decisions also happen without groupthink conditions prevailing, and groupthink can sometimes lead, luckily, to good outcomes. But Irving Janis's ideas have helped groups take steps to guard against the risks of groupthink in decision-making, such as leaders acting with impartiality, encouraging criticism, using devil's advocates, bringing outsiders in, and splitting groups up to examine all possible options.*

"CAN'T DO" ATTITUDE

THE MAIN CONCEPT | What happens if you spend your life in a society where everyone thinks that "people like you" are no good at something? The likelihood is, even if you work hard at it, when it comes down to make-or-break tests, something inside you will cause you to underperform. African-American psychologist Claude Steele termed this effect "stereotype threat," and explored its effects in a series of studies involving black students, who for decades had been negatively stereotyped intellectually. He was able to show (see opposite) that such stereotypes can have a damaging effect on performance in competitive situations, and since then researchers have shown this effect occurring widely with almost any group that experiences negative stereotyping. White American elite math students underperformed when tested alongside Asian-American students of exactly the same caliber, because the white students culturally considered themselves less skilled at math than their Asian colleagues. And the effect goes beyond the academic arena. In 1998, Jeff Stone and his colleagues asked elite athletes from the University of Arizona to compete in a ten-hole golf putting test. When it was presented as a test of natural athletic ability, white participants played a succession of bad shots and the black athletes performed better. When it was billed as a test of sport strategic intelligence, the result was the complete opposite.

THE EVIDENCE | In a 1995 study by Claude Steele and Joshua Aronson, a group of white and black Stanford University students were brought into the laboratory and given a very difficult 30-minute English literature test. In the "stereotype threat" condition, participants were told the paper was going to test verbal ability. In the "non-stereotype threat" condition, participants were told that the test paper was an instrument for studying problem-solving, and that it was "non-diagnostic" in terms of differences in ability between participants. The result was striking: black students performed significantly worse than their white colleagues when completing the test under the "threat" conditions. When black students completed the same test, but in the belief that it was not measuring ability, they performed at almost exactly the same levels as the white students.

THE WIDER PICTURE | *Globally, the biggest group of people who face stereotype threat are women—and in fact Claude Steele's earliest work on the subject centered on female university students taking math tests, whose performance improved when the sense of male-female rivalry was taken out. Stereotype threat has been shown to affect women in traditionally male domains (finance and banking, among many others), leading some to describe it as another form of "glass ceiling."*

CLAUDE STEELE BIOGRAPHY
Page 88
WE'RE NOT ALWAYS LIKE THIS
Page 126
INTELLIGENCE: A CAN OF WORMS
Page 130

IT'S ALWAYS US & THEM

THE MAIN CONCEPT | Every great sport, anywhere in the world, is guaranteed to produce some bitter sporting rivalries, and with these will be robust and probably unprintable chants about the opposition team. Singing these at full voice, in the stadium, with your friends, is what being a supporter is all about. It is also a good example of the kind of behavior predicted by Polish social psychologist Henri Tajfel's "social identity theory." Based at the University of Bristol, UK, in the 1970s, Tajfel was interested in why social groups discriminate against others. According to his theory, we all have a tendency to see people in terms of "us" and "them." The "us" part comes from our social identity—how we choose to be categorized within society. Given this, we start to draw favorable comparisons between us (our own group), and them (the relevant "out-groups"). In doing so, we play up similarities and positive aspects within our group, and tend to look unfavorably on the out-groups. The result, according to Tajfel, is that our self-esteem is boosted: think of how much fun it is to insult the opposing team! In Tajfel's theory, our idea of "self" gets identified with our group, and diminishing the out-group's self-esteem boosts our own. In the wider world beyond the sports stadium, the theory has been seen as an important framework for thinking about discrimination, prejudice, and intergroup conflict.

THE EVIDENCE | In 1970, Tajfel worked with teenage boys divided into two groups, apparently on the flimsiest of grounds (a preference for one painter or another, or the toss of a coin). The groups did not interact, nor did the boys know who was in their group or the other. When asked to allocate rewards (sums of money) to anonymous members of the two groups (but never to themselves), they showed systematic biases in giving more money to members of their own group than to the other. More tellingly, they also ignored choices that would have maximized money for both groups, choosing for both groups to end up less well-off, but to maximize the difference in earnings between the two (in their own group's favor, of course).

THE WIDER PICTURE | *Before social identity theory, there was a sense that group conflicts had to be driven by authoritarian personalities or else be "about" something—competing for jobs, for instance. What the theory tells us is that simply being put in a category is enough for us to get seriously biased in favor of our own groupings—and the more difference we can create, the better we feel.*

BEING IN SOMEONE ELSE'S SHOES
Page 78

HENRI TAJFEL BIOGRAPHY
Page 89

LOST IN THE CROWD
Page 110

MASLOW'S HIERARCHY

THE MAIN CONCEPT | Imagine you are a refugee, displaced from your homeland, walking with family members for days, exhausted, with few remaining possessions. What do you need most of all? Probably you crave food, clean water, rest, shelter, security: basic human needs. But once in a refugee center, you may then want to contact loved ones. This simple progression from needing the basics of survival through to concern for family and friends illustrates a part of what Abraham Maslow described in 1954 as the "hierarchy of needs." According to Maslow, we have an endless variety of needs, but not all at the same time. Instead, there is a rough order in play. Once basic needs are satisfied, we forget about them, and move up to the next set. So beyond food and shelter we want love and sense of belonging, and beyond this, we need respect and self-esteem. Then we seek knowledge and meaning, followed by aesthetic qualities like beauty and order. At the pinnacle is self-actualization—which Maslow describes as "realizing one's full potential." For him, this is a theory of human motivation: what we are striving for depends on what we have gained already. In reality, some people do not complete all these stages in strict order (people in refugee camps write poetry) and not everyone wants to. As for the summit of the hierarchy, the theory has prompted extensive research (see opposite) about what self-actualization really represents.

HUMANISTIC PSYCHOLOGY
Page 16

ERIKSON'S EIGHT STAGES OF MAN
Page 38

HOW TO BE IN THE ZONE
Page 80

THE EVIDENCE | Maslow attempted to characterize the pinnacle of the hierarchy of needs—self-actualization—by researching the lives and characteristics of people he regarded as having reached this pinnacle, and drawing out traits that he found in many of them. He selected a group of 18 people (including Abraham Lincoln, Albert Einstein, Mother Teresa, and Beethoven) and drew out 15 prevailing characteristics, including creativity, spontaneous thinking, ability to form deep relationships, and even a strong sense of humor. Here were the conditions for personal growth at the very highest level: what it takes to strive for perfection. In a more recent questionnaire-based study (2017), Jaimie Krems, Douglas Kenrick, and Rebecca Neel reported that among younger respondents and men, much of the drive toward realizing one's full potential comes from a desire simply for status: being seen to be exceptional, rather than actually being so.

THE WIDER PICTURE | *Maslow thought of the self-actualizing person (with examples such as Aldous Huxley and Mahatma Gandhi) "not as an ordinary man with something added, but rather as the ordinary man with nothing taken away." This idea, coupled with the work of Carl Rogers (pages 16–17), provided the springboard for the new science of humanistic psychology—and techniques for self-development promising to realize the full potential in all of us.*

SOCIAL LOAFING

THE MAIN CONCEPT | "Many hands make light work," the expression goes. Or do they? In 1913, French professor of agricultural engineering Max Ringelmann noticed that when a team of men combined forces on a rope-pulling task, each man pulled less weight than he could when acting alone. His findings were largely dismissed as being simply the result of the physical rope setup. Decades later, however, experimental interest in the phenomenon was rekindled. In 1979, Bibb Latané, Kipling Williams, and Stephen Harkins, who coined the term "social loafing," asked small groups of participants to create as much noise as possible for a lab experiment, but found that each individual made less noise in the group than when acting alone. Since then, there have been dozens of variations on this kind of experiment, all leading to similar results, whether it be rope-pulling, swimming (see opposite), songwriting, or navigating a maze. There are several theories as to why this happens. Some are based on the way that external pressure to perform (the boss's expectations, for example) ends up being diffused across the whole group, somehow weakening it and in turn reducing the drive to perform. Other theories relate to the ability to hide within the group, or to disengage— sensing that one's performance is not essential to the success of the task. We've all been there.

THE EVIDENCE | Kipling Williams, Steve Nida, Lawrence Baca, and Bibb Latané—along with Ohio State University swimming coach Dick Sloan—staged a swimming gala, invited spectators to cheer on the teams, and offered prizes. They claimed to be studying race-starting techniques and water-turbulence effects, but were really exploring social loafing: would athletes swim faster times in individual races than in the relay? There was a crucial variable involved. In some relay races, swimmers' individual times would be called out to the teams and spectators, while in others they would not. The experimenters found that where individual performances were not communicated, performance was reduced. Social loafing, then, was happening in the pool, as well as in the lab.

THE WIDER PICTURE | *When Latané, Williams, and Harkins first described social loafing, they went so far as to call it a "social disease." In 1995, however, Williams and Steven Karau showed that social loafing can be avoided. Much depends on how much the individual cares about the group's objectives, how valued the individual feels, and what they can expect to get out of it. Selfish, maybe, but effective.*

ACHIEVEMENT MOTIVATION
Page 50
THE BYSTANDER EFFECT
Page 98
LOST IN THE CROWD
Page 110

LOST IN THE CROWD

THE MAIN CONCEPT | In August 2011, neighborhoods in London and elsewhere in the UK were hit by night after night of looting and burning. Mobs of people, quite literally, "ran riot." In the aftermath, many of the perpetrators, caught on CCTV, appeared in court; they included a chef, an elementary school teacher, an opera steward, and a millionaire's daughter. Many were at a loss to explain their behavior. Back in 1895, in an influential book entitled *The Crowd*, French philosopher Gustave Le Bon had written that when someone joins a crowd that shares a common goal, he stops acting as individual: "He is no longer himself, but has become an automaton who has ceased to be guided by his will." Le Bon's ideas on mob mentality have been nuanced and developed since—for example by Philip Zimbardo (pages 96–97), who in 1969 suggested that people in crowds can be "deindividuated"—losing their sense of personal identity, and allowing themselves to act in ways that are more extreme or lawless than they would if acting alone. This idea was extended in 1979 by American psychologist Ed Diener, who believed that being subsumed by the mob identity leaves us prone to uninhibited, impulsive, and uncontrolled behavior; a loss of capacity to think or plan rationally; and a heightened emotional sensitivity to the events around us—all of which was evident on those hot August nights.

THE EVIDENCE | In 1979, Diener recreated "deindividuation" in a lab setting. He studied a group of eight people, of whom just two were genuine participants, and six were "confederates" in on the act. From the outset, the group was friendly, chose a name for itself, and had fun getting dressed for the tasks ahead. They then sang songs, linked arms for a game, and danced to loud African drumming music—clapping and swaying, with the lights dimmed. Faced with a choice of activities afterward, this deindividuated group showed a strong preference for "disinhibited" tasks like playing in mud or "painting with your nose." Meanwhile, participants in groups that had been prepared differently—to maximize their sense of self-awareness, for example—picked "inhibited" activities such as doing crosswords or reading.

THE WIDER PICTURE | *In 1986, Jane Siegel and colleagues presciently identified another realm where deindividuating effects could play out: what they called, at the time, "computer-mediated communications," but what today we might call social media. The online troll's sense of anonymity, with their identity subsumed within an emotional online "crowd," seems to be a recipe for disinhibition, extreme arguments, and impulsive, uncontrolled behavior.*

EVIL IN THE BEST OF US
Page 96

IT'S ALWAYS US & THEM
Page 104

SOCIAL LOAFING
Page 108

THE BEAUTY BIAS

THE MAIN CONCEPT | "What is beautiful is good." So said the Greek poet Sappho, some 2,500 years ago. And the link between physical attractiveness and all manner of moral attributes, captured in that fragment of poetry, remains a potent one even today. In 1972, in what has become a classic study on the subject, Karen Dion, Ellen Berscheid, and Elaine Walster (see opposite) demonstrated the pervasive stereotype of physical attractiveness. Not only were physically attractive people assumed to possess more socially desirable personalities than less physically attractive people, it was also assumed that they would lead happier and more successful lives. This bias toward beauty starts early. In 1987, Judith Langlois showed how babies seem to prefer pictures of women rated as "attractive" to those rated as "unattractive." And the idea of beauty and goodness is embedded in children's culture, from fairy tales (the handsome prince, the ugly sisters) through to some of the biggest (though less recent) Disney movies, as a 2010 paper by Denise Martz and colleagues revealed. Back in 1977, Judith Langlois and Cookie Stephan had also found that older children shown photos of other children picked out the attractive-looking ones as more likely to be good playmates, friendlier, and better at sharing. The effect seems to be ingrained—and reinforced—throughout our lives.

GENDER IDENTITY
Page 48

BEING IN SOMEONE ELSE'S SHOES
Page 78

IT'S ALWAYS US & THEM
Page 104

THE EVIDENCE | For their study, Dion, Berscheid, and Walster enlisted a group of 60 student participants (30 males and 30 females) to view a series of photographs of other young adults, on the pretext that this was an experiment to test the accuracy of their "person perception" over a long-term study of the individuals concerned. Unknown to the group, the faces in the photographs had been previously ranked as "unattractive," "average," and "attractive." The participants were invited to assign values for various attributes to each person, including how sociable they were likely to be, their occupational status, "marital competence," and their social and professional happiness. Participants rated "attractive" individuals more favorably than the others across all criteria.

THE WIDER PICTURE | *The idea that what is beautiful is good is ingrained in Western culture from childhood up. The other side of this is the assumption that what is not beautiful is bad—ushering in self-image problems that can affect all ages. In a 2013 article on the subject, Iris Vermeir and Dieneke Van de Sompel called for schools to teach children to ditch the stereotype—and for filmmakers to demonstrate that "what is less beautiful" can be good, too.*

LOVE IN THE LAB

THE MAIN CONCEPT | Nothing has been written about, contemplated, or discussed more than the nature of human relationships. Around the time of the 1967 "Summer of Love," psychologist Arthur Aron, a graduate student at the University of California, Berkeley, fell in love with Elaine Spaulding—later known as Elaine Aron, his wife and collaborator on a social psychology career spanning five decades. Aron recalls that he fell in love "very intensely" and was curious to see what research existed on the subject. There was hardly anything, so he decided to take on the topic of love himself. In an interview following his now-famous 1997 study using university students in a lab setting—popularly known as "The 36 Questions That Lead to Love" (see opposite)—Aron stated that the psychological study of intimacy is critical: "It is the biggest predictor of relationship quality, and of human happiness—more than wealth or success. And it's a huge predictor of health." In fact, how long we live, he found, is more strongly influenced by relationship quality than by factors such as smoking or obesity. So what is it exactly that makes us feel close to someone else? A key pattern, as suggested in 1973 by Irwin Altman and Dalmas Taylor, seems to be sustained, escalating, and personal self-disclosure over a period of time—and this is exactly what Aron and his colleagues set out to do in a lab setting using university students in the mid-1990s.

THE EVIDENCE | Billed as a study of "interpersonal closeness," male and female university students were "matched" in pairs (based on an attitude survey) and then left alone to take turns asking and answering a set of 36 questions. These began with a question about the ideal dinner guest, and became increasingly personal, exploring participants' worst memories, inviting them to share important facts about themselves, and later, to tell the other "something you like about them already." The sequence concluded with the instruction to look into each other's eyes for four minutes. The high post-experiment ratings of closeness and anecdotal reports of the impact the experiment had on the participants showed that it was a success in sparking intimacy between people. One pair from the initial experiment even got married.

THE WIDER PICTURE | *The study went on to gain wide popularity in popular culture, with the appearance of countless articles and podcasts in which people confess that the 36 questions have led them to start a long-term relationship with their partner. The 36 questions have also been used in experiments to initiate friendships across a cultural divide, and to examine and break down prejudice and tension between social groups.*

IT'S ALWAYS US & THEM
Page 104

MASLOW'S HIERARCHY
OF NEEDS
Page 106

THE BEAUTY BIAS
Page 112

"This is encouraging evidence of the power of the environment to influence characteristics like intelligence. Even if traits like intelligence have large genetic determinants, they are still substantially malleable."

WALTER MISCHEL,
THE MARSHMALLOW TEST (2014)

4

PSYCHOLOGY OF DIFFERENCE

INTRODUCTION

This final chapter explores individual differences, including personality, intelligence, and the concept of mental health. We consider early personality psychology, dating back to the Middle Ages when bodily fluids (blood, phlegm, and bile) were seen as driving differences in character, and phrenology, a nineteenth-century concept, which located dozens of character traits in discrete pockets within the brain, and which, through careful measurement, could be found on the contours of the skull (pages 122–23). By the turn of the twentieth century, Freud was developing his psychoanalytic theory of the human mind, which saw certain aspects of what we could call neurotic and psychotic personalities as being the results of instinctual drives, repressed conflicts, and unconscious desires. For Freud, the expression of our personality was the result of an inner struggle between our basic instinct to seek pleasure (the id), our controlling and rather persecutory conscience (the super-ego), and our ego itself, trying to match up our inner world with the real world.

Testing and measuring

While psychoanalysis provided a route to explore certain neurotic behaviors, it had little to say about differences in personality between "healthy" individuals—what they were like, and how they might behave. A demand for this kind of assessment grew up with wartime conscription to filter out "unsuitable" applicants, and from this developed increasingly complex attempts to narrow down aspects of personality into something that could be applied and measured universally.

We can briefly summarize the milestones in this work (pages 124–25). In the 1930s, Gordon Allport took a dictionary and listed 4,504 words that described aspects of personality, eventually narrowing his list down to 161 separate and universal character traits. Later work by Raymond Cattell and, separately, by Hans J. Eysenck, used a statistical technique called factor analysis (which filters out traits that always seemed to be correlated) to distill personality traits further. Cattell thus came up with 16 pairs of traits—the famous 16PF personality test. Eysenck, using a different conceptual framework, developed his EPQ test, which settled on three major factors.

By the 1980s, the prevailing model had broadened out to the "Big Five" model (pages 126–27), which has proved enduring and popular. However, there has been an ongoing debate about whether trait personality theories can predict a person's behavior in all situations. If traits only apply in some situations, then how accurate and useful is a personality trait in the first place? In fact, as Walter Mischel proposes, it is possible to think of a personality trait as a kind of "if … then" idea—so that a certain kind of trait will apply in a certain kind of situation. For example: "If I am under pressure, then I will act impulsively." Mischel's famous experiment with marshmallows showed that a person's power of self-control can be learned—so that the extent to which our typical behaviors are influenced by a situation will depend on how we perceive the situation, and what we have learned about self-control (pages 128–29). The result has been to create somewhat more nuanced ideas of what a trait is. If someone is aggressive when anxious, but convivial when relaxed, this in itself can be seen as a good predictor of behavior in those two situations. Beyond this, the cognitive and social aspects that drive that anxiety can be worked on, so we are not locked into exactly the same behavior patterns for the rest of our lives.

What's normal, anyway?

This chapter also explores the concept of nature and nurture in relation to measures of intelligence (pages 130–31). One way of unpicking this complex issue is to think of genetic factors—some neural structure in the brain—as sometimes leading us to react to situations in a certain way. Whether we do or not depends on environmental, social, cultural, or cognitive factors that influence whether that genetic disposition is expressed, or not. Exceptional talent has often been seen as some kind of genetic gift, putting it at the "nature" end of the nature/nurture debate. To round off our treatment of personality difference, we explore Anders Ericsson's view that talent is not about being gifted, but is all down to relentless practice (pages 132–33).

The chapter ends by looking at psychology's view on what is normal and abnormal, with perspectives on some common mental health issues. Categorizing mental illnesses is a problematic process; signals and symptoms can easily be misinterpreted, as David Rosenhan demonstrated in 1973 (pages 134–35) with his "pseudopatients" admitted to psychiatric wards. Most theorists have concluded that key aspects of mental "abnormality" are distress and an inability to get on with one's life—although an element of social judgment (pages 136–37) of what is acceptable is always at the heart of certain illness definitions. On specific illness, we look at Martin Seligman's influential theory on "learned helplessness" as a component of clinical depression (pages 138–39), some recent thinking about eating disorders (pages 140–41), schizophrenia's debilitating "negative" symptoms (pages 142–43), the inner tyranny faced by sufferers of obsessive compulsive disorder (pages 144–45), and, finally, the strange and rare instances of dissociative identity disorder (pages 146–47).

BIOGRAPHIES

GORDON ALLPORT (1897–1967)

Born in Indiana, Allport became a pioneer of research on human personality, as well as an influential theorist on group prejudice and race relations. The son of a devout Methodist mother and a physician father, he was raised with the values of "good character" and a strong work ethic. He won a scholarship to Harvard in 1915, and spent time volunteering in community projects and teaching English in Istanbul before completing a psychology Ph.D. in 1922. Interested in the new field of personality psychology from the outset, he published *Personality Traits* in 1921 with his brother Floyd (also a psychologist), and taught one of the United States' first courses on the subject in 1922. He joined the Harvard faculty in 1930 and remained for his entire career. His 1937 *Personality: A Psychological Interpretation* established traits as a basic unit of personality— a dramatic departure from the behaviorism prevailing in the United States and the psychoanalytic approach in Europe. Allport tackled big social issues, researching the power of rumor during the war years, and later theorizing about religious belief. He is best known for *The Nature of Prejudice* (1954), which included the Allport Scale of Prejudice—describing forms of prejudice in society, from hate speech to discrimination and, ultimately, extermination.

RAYMOND CATTELL (1905–1998)

Cattell was born near Birmingham, UK. The first in his family to attend university, he gained a first class degree in chemistry before switching to psychology, partly influenced by a lecture he attended by Cyril Burt (a pioneer in intelligence testing and theory), which helped to define Cattell's future career. He completed his Ph.D. in London in 1929, and moved to the US in 1937 to work as a research associate at Columbia University, later becoming a professor of psychology at Clark, then (at the invitation of Gordon Allport) a lecturer at Harvard. After the war he founded the Laboratory of Personality Assessment at the University of Illinois, where he remained for 27 years, leading research on personality trait measures using a statistical tool called "factor analysis"—made possible in part by the university's sophisticated in-house computer, a rarity at the time. *Personality: A Systematic, Theoretical, and Factual Study* (1950) was the first of Cattell's several influential books in this field and he developed dozens of testing programs, including the famous 16 Personality Factor Questionnaire. Over his lifetime, he published 43 books and 575 articles, and wrote widely about personality, intelligence, evolution, genetics, and a new religion that he called "Beyondism."

HANS EYSENCK (1916–1997)

Eysenck was born in Berlin, the son of a cabaret entertainer and his actress wife. Raised by his grandmother following his parents' divorce, he left Germany for the UK in the 1930s—in opposition to the Nazi party—and completed his psychology Ph.D. in London in 1940. During the war he became a research psychologist at the Mill Hill military psychiatric unit outside London, remaining with the unit as it relocated to its London base, where he became its director of psychology, and shortly afterward, professor of psychology with the affiliated new Institute of Psychiatry. Eysenck went beyond analyzing and defining personality traits to develop a theory of personality, searching for neurobiological factors that could influence personality, leading to the 1957 publication of *The Dynamics of Anxiety and Hysteria* , and ten years later, *The Biological Basis of Personality*, where he elaborated on the idea that "cortical arousal" is a determinant of introvert/extrovert personality differences. Eysenck was a prolific writer within the professional field of psychology as well as in popular science and self-help, and his fearless and nonconformist approach generated controversy throughout his career.

WALTER MISCHEL (1930–2018)

Mischel was born in Vienna, but following the Nazi annexation of Austria in 1938, his family emigrated to the United States. He won a scholarship to New York University in 1951, then went on to gain a Ph.D. in psychology at Ohio State in 1956 (which included a study of tribal rituals in Trinidad, which sparked a lifelong interest in studies of self-control). Much of his academic life was spent at Stanford, whose Bing Nursery School was the venue for the famous "marshmallow test." His 1968 book *Personality and Assessment* challenged the assumptions of trait theory—which looked for lasting traits—and shifted the agenda toward situations, or so-called "if ... then" personality traits. This led to Mischel and Yuichi Shoda's Cognitive Affective Personality System (CAPS) to model interactions between persons and situations. While the expression of traits is influenced by situations, the effect of situations can in turn be mitigated by self-control, which is something that can be learned. Mischel and Shoda showed how "hot" temptations can be "cooled" to create more self-control—and how strong self-control predicts better outcomes later in life. Mischel was the Niven Professor of Humane Letters in Psychology at Columbia University until 2017.

WHERE IS IT KEPT?

THE MAIN CONCEPT | Since the beginning of time, we have tried to understand why people are like they are—or more specifically, why we are all so different from each other. The Greek physician Galen talked of the human psyche as an intellectual "charioteer" trying to manage our (at times unruly) driving forces of intentions and emotions. Another Greek idea remained popular through and beyond the Middle Ages: the concept of the four "humors." These were effectively bodily fluids—blood, phlegm, and two types of bile, with one or other affecting the balance of our personality. By the beginning of the nineteenth century, a new model of personality emerged—phrenology, which shifted the focus to the brain (mainly the skull) and speculated that our personality traits depend on how far certain parts of that organ are developed, with different zones dealing with specific faculties (like "secretiveness" just above the ear, and "combativeness" just behind it). Phrenologists would even measure bumps on patients' skulls as a guide to identifying these traits. The more accurate idea that parts of the brain have specific functions arrived later in the century, by which time physicians such as Paul Broca and David Ferrier had found sites within the brain associated with language and emotion. Only then could they start to make sense of the personalities of brain-damaged individuals such as Phineas Gage (see opposite).

THE EVIDENCE | In 1848 Phineas Gage, age 25, was the foreman on the construction of a railroad in Vermont. In a traumatic accident while blasting through a rock face, a long iron rod pierced his left cheekbone and passed right through the left side of his brain, exiting the top of his skull and landing some distance behind him. Thanks to exceptional medical care from a Dr. John Harlow, Gage survived, remaining active and reasonably healthy for the next 11 years. But his personality was dramatically changed. From being a well-balanced, sociable, and prudent man, he became impulsive, irritable, and crude. Gage's case became much discussed as evidence of the physiological roots—within the brain matter—of our personality traits.

THE BIRTH OF QUESTIONNAIRES
Page 124

WE'RE NOT ALWAYS LIKE THIS
Page 126

WORK IN PROGRESS
Page 128

THE WIDER PICTURE | *The dramatic shift from the long-standing "humor" model to the idea that personalities are in some way linked to our brains showed how science was slowly closing in on the mysteries of personality. But while the study of brain injuries provided evidence that some broad aspects of our behavior are controlled by specific parts of the brain, it left a big question unanswered: why we are all so different from each other?*

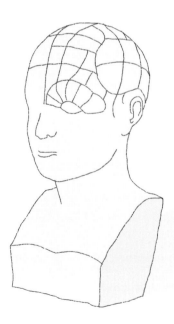

THE BIRTH OF QUESTIONNAIRES

THE MAIN CONCEPT | "Discover Yourself!" "Find Out Your Type!" The web is full of invitations to complete online personality tests. In fact, today's questionnaires are part of eight decades of research into personality traits—descriptions used to assess, and explain, human behavior. Early researchers first set about deciding which traits to measure. In 1936, Gordon Allport and Henry Odbert pored over a dictionary and chose 4,504 words that described personality—terms that had been in use for centuries. Stripping out synonyms and little-used words, they edited this down to 161 traits—still too many to test with a questionnaire. British psychologist Raymond Cattell later refined their long list down to just 16 pairs of opposites (such as calm-irritable), which eventually led to Cattell's "16 Personality Factor" (or 16PF) personality test. Meanwhile in the UK, Hans Eysenck distilled personality down to just two dimensions from which many other behaviors could be derived: neuroticism ("N"), including anxiety, tension, and other negative emotional states on a scale from "stable" to "unstable"; and extraversion ("E"), with a scale from quiet, passive introverts to sociable, active extroverts. In 1978 he added a third—psychoticism ("P"), which measures aspects of aggression, self-centeredness, and empathy. All three come together in the EPQ—the Eysenck Personality Questionnaire.

THE EVIDENCE | Eysenck believed that the EPQ would be a good predictor of certain behaviors, including criminality, with offender populations scoring high on neuroticism, extraversion, and psychoticism (showing up as impulsive, aggressive, excitable, and somewhat cold-blooded). In 1981, Philippe Rushton and Roland Chrisjohn studied school children and older students and found a close correlation between these personality factors and delinquent behavior. However, in studies of actual convicted offenders, many scored highly on P and N traits as predicted, but results on the extraversion traits were inconclusive—possibly because this is both a measure of sociability (which many delinquents lack) as well as impulsiveness (which they have). For some, the EPQ can seem just a little too compact.

GORDON ALLPORT, RAYMOND CATTELL, HANS EYSENCK BIOGRAPHIES
Pages 120–21

WE'RE NOT ALWAYS LIKE THIS
Page 126

WORK IN PROGRESS
Page 128

THE WIDER PICTURE | *For Eysenck, differences in personality were mainly the result of genetic factors. Extroverts, he believed, had uncomfortably low levels of brainwave activity, so outgoing behavior was a means of getting what we might call "more of a buzz" (and vice versa for introverts). This has never been proven scientifically, but studies of twins do show that around 40 percent of our personality traits may have a genetic origin. What the mechanism is, though, remains elusive.*

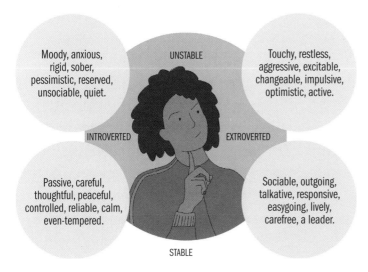

Moody, anxious, rigid, sober, pessimistic, reserved, unsociable, quiet.

UNSTABLE

Touchy, restless, aggressive, excitable, changeable, impulsive, optimistic, active.

INTROVERTED

EXTROVERTED

Passive, careful, thoughtful, peaceful, controlled, reliable, calm, even-tempered.

Sociable, outgoing, talkative, responsive, easygoing, lively, carefree, a leader.

STABLE

WE'RE NOT ALWAYS LIKE THIS

THE MAIN CONCEPT | While the quest for a reliable (and short) list of traits that can describe the vast range of human personalities has been around for decades, a kind of consensus has emerged around the so-called "Big Five" personality traits. This is the result of research from several independent studies and statistical analysis of existing trait models (by Warren Norman in 1963, Robert McCrae and Paul Costa in 1985, and Patricia Noller and colleagues in 1987). The Big Five begins with the two main planks of Eysenck's trait model—extraversion and neuroticism (page 124), then builds in three more elements: conscientiousness (including aspects of dependability and trustworthiness), agreeableness (including willingness to criticize others), and "openness to experience" (measuring curiosity, creativity, and imagination). The Big Five has become a widely used personality model, but like all such "trait" models, has one specific limitation. Walter Mischel has shown that our traits vary depending on the situation they are in—someone terrified by the dentist may be a courageous rock climber—so simply describing someone as "sociable" or "reserved" is misleading. Mischel's research (see opposite) led to the "if ... then" profile: situation-based personality patterns, such as: "If she is at the dentist, then she will be anxious" or "If she is rock climbing, then she will be calm."

THE EVIDENCE | In 1994, Yuichi Schoda, Walter Mischel, and Jack Wright made a six-week study of boys at a summer camp, comparing behaviors in various interpersonal situations: being teased or provoked by a peer; being warned, punished, or praised by an adult; and being approached socially by a peer. The boys' behaviors (aggression, withdrawal, friendliness, and so on) were recorded relative to each situation, with an average of 167 hours of observation time per child. This enormous dataset allowed the researchers to see exactly how each boy's behavior changed depending on the situation, and to observe how boys consistently switched behavior patterns in certain situations. The results provided strong evidence that participants' "if … then" personality profiles were both distinct and stable.

THE WIDER PICTURE | *While situations drive our behavior, the "agreeableness" trait in the Big Five model can also play a part. Those scoring very high in agreeableness sometimes show what Mark Snyder in 1987 labeled "self-monitoring" behavior. At the extreme, they become almost a different person, depending on who they are with. A fictional example of this is the character Leonard Zelig ("Chameleon Man") played by Woody Allen in his 1983 movie,* Zelig.

BARON-COHEN & AUTISM
Page 46

WALTER MISCHEL BIOGRAPHY
Page 121

WORK IN PROGRESS
Page 128

WORK IN PROGRESS

THE MAIN CONCEPT | Are you a glass-half-full or a glass-half-empty kind of person? Whatever your answer, can you think why that might be so? In contrast to the trait theories of personality (which might simply label you as "optimistic" or "pessimistic"), there is another kind of personality theory that puts learning, experience, and "self-efficacy" (an ability to control what happens to us) at the heart of personality development. Pessimists may feel that prior experiences suggest a given situation is not looking good and is probably out of their control— low self-efficacy beliefs. This way of thinking about personality (social cognitive theory) is based on Albert Bandura's social learning theory (pages 40–41), which is all about observing and imitating role models, and forming expectations. Also important is our capacity for self-regulation—controlling our desires and actions, which includes judging ourselves and feeling pride or shame. These facets, taken together, explain a whole range of behaviors. So where you might appear to be "impulsive" on a trait-based personality test, this is simply based on your assessment of your behavior right now. In other situations and over time, you may learn—through various experiences, including acquiring self-control (see opposite)—to be less impulsive. The interplay between behavior, environment, beliefs, and emotions gives us the capacity to develop and change. Nothing, in the terms of this theory, is set in stone.

BARON-COHEN & AUTISM
Page 46

WALTER MISCHEL BIOGRAPHY
Page 121

WE'RE NOT ALWAYS LIKE THIS
Page 126

THE EVIDENCE | In 1960, Walter Mischel began a set of experiments at a Stanford nursery school with 653 four-year-olds. Researchers sat a child in front of a treat—a marshmallow, for instance—and then left the child alone. If the child did not consume the treat, they would earn two treats when the researcher returned. If they couldn't wait, they earned just one treat. Mischel discovered—from 50 years of subsequent studies as his subjects grew up—that children who were able to delay gratification went on to lead more successful lives. But crucially, this ability to self-regulate could be learned: "hot" emotional drives that lead us to want to act can actually be "cooled" by thinking in a certain way—in this example, by imagining the marshmallow is a picture, rather than a real candy.

THE WIDER PICTURE | *Social cognitive theory acknowledges that our personalities are shaped by our environments, families, parents, or even what we see on TV, and that the idea of being able to influence or control our outcomes is also a key factor: self-control can be learned. But beyond what we are able to observe and learn, there are wild cards like emotions and genetics that keep the mysteries of personality as difficult to crack as they ever were.*

INTELLIGENCE: A CAN OF WORMS

THE MAIN CONCEPT | Ever since Alfred Binet and Theodore Simon developed the first IQ test in 1905, the measurement of intelligence, and the differences in IQ that have been observed, have been the source of heated debate and endless controversy. Binet and Simon devised the test to create a snapshot of a child's learning, to highlight which aspects of development needed to be worked on. But the test (and its successors) fast became an indication of one's lifelong intellectual potential, and a means of making differences in intellect appear as undeniable as differences in height or weight. This hazardous tool became part of the weaponry of the eugenics movement, and the vision of selectively breeding a superior race of humans—with disastrous consequences. Since then, IQ tests have become more sophisticated, but they have survived as a constant unit of measure in the search for the origins (genetic, environmental) of our intelligence, despite concerns about whether such tests discriminate against certain cultures or groups. Many studies involving identical twins separated at birth, or children in adoption, have been used to supply evidence for the "intelligence is genetic" argument, or indeed to try to prove the opposite: that environment is key. Eric Turkheimer and colleagues (see opposite) carried out a study that showed that both nature and nurture play a part; it all depends on your family circumstances.

THE EVIDENCE | In 2003, Eric Turkheimer and colleagues studied 320 pairs of twins using extensive data from a national survey of newborn infants carried out in the 1960s, which included details of their socio-economic status and IQ scores. Using sophisticated computer analysis, they discovered that in the most impoverished families, the home environment had by far the biggest influence (around 60 percent) on differences between IQ scores. But in more affluent families, the opposite was true: genetics had the biggest influence. The implication is that improving conditions for the very poorest children in society could help them to "unlock" their IQ potential. Whereas for children who enjoy an "adequate" level of living conditions, how smart they are appears to be much more down to their genes.

THE WIDER PICTURE | *The old nature/nurture debates assumed that nature—your genes—gives you your intelligence, and then, separately, your environment can help you add to this. These days, the two appear as completely intertwined: your genetic makeup will help determine what you make of your environment, but equally, your environment will have an effect on how far your genetic makeup can be activated or expressed.*

ACHIEVEMENT MOTIVATION
Page 50

"CAN'T DO" ATTITUDE
Page 102

HARD GRAFT OR GENIUS?
Page 132

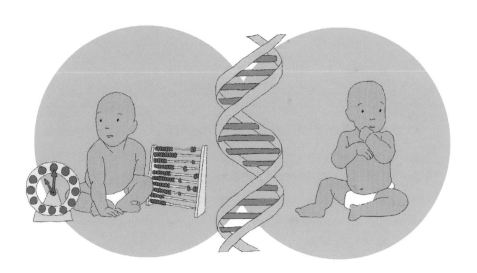

HARD GRAFT OR GENIUS?

THE MAIN CONCEPT | Fed up with your job? Want to become a concert pianist instead? If you do three hours of serious practice per day for the next ten years, you might just make it. The idea that exceptional talent, or genius, can simply be worked at, is controversial. Francis Galton, in his 1869 book *Hereditary Genius*, analyzed genealogical records of eminent musicians, artists, and writers, and found that for many, talent appeared to run in the family. By contrast, behaviorist thinkers such as John B. Watson (page 12), writing in the early twentieth century, believed that anyone could be taught to excel, regardless of their background. In 1993, research by the Swedish psychologist Anders Ericsson and others appeared to support this view—suggesting that exceptional talent, such as we see in musicians, really is simply down to rigorous practice rather than any kind of personality traits, and that, on average, it takes 10,000 hours to become an international-level pianist. Ericsson's findings prompted a succession of challenges. In 2014 David Hambrick and others studied chess players and found that talent did seem to be a factor, as was innate intelligence. In music, too, further research has shown that some students need less practice than others, suggesting there is something else involved, while the age at which people start learning also matters. So on second thoughts, maybe stick to the day job?

THE EVIDENCE | In 1993, Anders Ericsson, Ralf Krampe, and Clemens Tesch-Romer made a study of violin students, teachers, and professional violinists at a German music academy, looking at practice hours and factors such as sleep and leisure patterns. One of the most telling results was how many practice hours, on average, members of each of these four groups had accumulated by the age of 18. The best student violinists had put in an average of 7,410 practice hours, whereas the "good" students had an average of 5,301 hours. The music teachers had each completed an average of 3,420 hours of practice by 18, whereas the professionals had a similar total to that of the best students. An extension of the study on pianists came up with similar outcomes.

THE WIDER PICTURE | *Rather like the nature/nurture question, the idea of whether a genius is born or created has been portrayed as a somewhat binary choice between two competing factors. Ericsson acknowledged that a "tenacity" trait was also a factor. Beyond that, there may also be environmental factors that answer the question of why some of us are driven to succeed in the first place.*

ACHIEVEMENT MOTIVATION
Page 50

HOW TO BE IN THE ZONE
Page 80

INTELLIGENCE: A CAN OF WORMS
Page 130

ON BEING SANE IN INSANE PLACES

THE MAIN CONCEPT | When we talk about a mental "disorder" what do we mean? The idea of a standardized diagnosis goes back to 1913, when German psychiatrist Emil Kraepelin drew up his influential classifications of mental illness. He proposed five distinct types: functional psychoses, which involve a disconnection with reality, and include what today are known as schizophrenia and bipolar disorder; neuroses, which are mainly driven by uncontrollable anxiety; personality disorders, including psychopathy, obsessive disorders, and paranoia; organic psychoses—caused by neurological diseases; and what was called "mental retardation." Kraepelin looked at a patient's symptoms, and on that basis, gave their illness a category—a process that underpinned medical psychiatry, and still does, in the form of today's *Diagnostic and Statistical Manual of Mental Disorders* (the DSM). But by the mid-twentieth century, it was clear that this practice can be highly subjective—allowing scope for enormous variations. These concerns led an experiment by David Rosenhan in 1973 (see opposite) that observed "normal" patients in a psychiatric ward. For Rosenhan, psychiatric diagnosis was unreliable, too easily influenced by the environment where the patient was seen: the "bizarre setting" of the psychiatric ward could provoke unusual behavior in anyone, or make normal behavior look bizarre.

THE BIRTH OF QUESTIONNAIRES
Page 124

NORMALITY: WHO'S THE JUDGE?
Page 136

SHUTTERED BY SCHIZOPHRENIA
Page 142

THE EVIDENCE | In his 1973 paper "On Being Sane in Insane Places," David Rosenhan described how he arranged for eight healthy volunteer "pseudopatients" (including himself) to be admitted to different psychiatric hospitals after (falsely) telling doctors they had been hearing voices. Once admitted, the eight behaved completely normally, but nonetheless, were treated by unwitting hospital staff as if they were ill. When volunteers took notes during the experiment, nursing staff described this "engaging in writing behavior" as if it were part of their symptoms. And the case history of one volunteer was written up by a doctor in such a way as to make an everyday family history appear dramatically pathological. All eight were eventually discharged (some after several weeks), diagnosed as suffering from schizophrenia in remission.

THE WIDER PICTURE | *Rosenhan followed up with another study that involved genuinely ill people admitted to psychiatric wards, where staff were warned that as part of an experiment, some may be "normal" rather than ill. Hospital staff rated large numbers of the ill participants to be "normal" when in fact they were suffering from mental illness. Rosenhan's work prompted searching questions over the US mental health system—and led to eventual improvements.*

NORMALITY: WHO'S THE JUDGE?

THE MAIN CONCEPT | The idea of what is normal and what is not is a thorny issue, because a part of what makes up "normal" behavior is linked with what society around us judges acceptable. In psychology, the most helpful way of thinking about abnormality is when it describes ways in which someone's life can be adversely affected—so it prevents someone just getting on with life. In their influential book *Abnormal Psychology* (1989), David Rosenhan and Martin Seligman proposed a set of seven criteria for abnormality. The first four are "suffering" (though some abnormal people, such as psychopaths, may appear not to suffer); "maladaptiveness"—an inability to hold down relationships, say, or a steady job; "irrationality and incomprehensibility"—behaving in a way that seems impossible to understand; and fourthly, behaviors that seem unpredictable and without control. The latter three link with society's views on what should count as "normal" behavior (see opposite) and include "vivid and unconventional behavior," "observer discomfort," and "a violation of moral and ideal standards." In 2001, in a different approach, Ronald Comer usefully identified four central features of abnormality—arriving at what have become known as "the four Ds": deviance, distress, dysfunction, and danger. Any of these could signal the need for medical or therapeutic help. But equally, any of these could be an aspect of normal behavior, too.

THE UNIVERSALITY OF THE EMOJI
Page 70

ON BEING SANE IN INSANE PLACES
Page 134

SHUTTERED BY SCHIZOPHRENIA
Page 142

THE EVIDENCE | In 1981, Olayiwola Erinosho and Akolawole Ayonrinde conducted a study in Nigeria with 771 respondents from both rural and urban areas, exploring peoples' knowledge and opinions of descriptions of people meeting Western classifications as having mental illness, including schizophrenia, paranoid schizophrenia, and anxiety/depression. Would people recognize certain symptomatic behavior patterns as being those of people with a mental illness? And would they be prepared to live, work with, or marry people matching those descriptions? The findings showed that substantial portions of both literate city dwellers and nonliterate rural communities did not associate the range of described behaviors with being those of someone with a mental illness. Instead, a majority of both the rural and urban samples saw the symptoms as simply antisocial behaviors—rather than illnesses to be treated.

THE WIDER PICTURE | *At best, we might think about the concepts of normal and abnormal as being at either end of a continuum. This though is a sliding scale on which the measuring points are ill-defined and are being influenced by the kind of culture that we live in.*

SELIGMAN & DEPRESSION

THE MAIN CONCEPT | Depression of one kind or another can hit almost all of us. Anyone who has encountered it, or been close to people suffering it, will be familiar with the symptoms, and their effects. "Clinical" depression is diagnosed when someone encounters at least five out of a list of eight symptoms, more or less daily, for a period of at least two weeks. Here is the complete list: low mood, a loss of pleasure from one's activities, interrupted sleep, weight loss or gain, loss of energy, low self-worth, an inability to concentrate, and thoughts of dying or suicide. Beyond these specific symptoms, many people with depression have a sense of helplessness—that there is nothing that can be done to change the situation they are in. Where does this mindset come from? American psychologist Martin Seligman believes that it's learned through a set of experiences that leads people to conclude that nothing they do will improve their situation—a common belief among depressed people. Seligman and others later refined this to show that this helplessness is affected by the meaning people ascribe to past events. This is a similar approach to work on depression by Aaron T. Beck (pages 68–69), who noted how depressed people's thinking is dominated by negative thoughts about one's self (seen as inadequate), the world (full of insurmountable obstacles), and the future (which will never improve).

THE EVIDENCE | Martin Seligman and Steven Maier were first-year graduate students at Pennsylvania University in 1964—a time when testing dogs with uncomfortable electric shocks in a lab was still commonplace. They noticed that if dogs learned to operate a lever to stop the shock, then they would subsequently learn—in a second experiment—to jump out of a box to escape the electric shock. But if the dogs found that whatever they did to the lever, there was no way it would stop the shock, then in the second experiment, even though they could have jumped out of the box if they wanted to, they just lay down and accepted the electric shocks. The futility of trying and failing had led in turn to a kind of apathy, or "learned helplessness."

THE WIDER PICTURE | *A tendency toward negative thinking can of course exist in people who never get depressed, but almost always appears in people who do get depressed. This suggests that there are other factors that can trigger the illness. Life event studies (such as those of George Brown and Tirril Harris in 1978) suggest that a significant loss, coupled with a sense of social isolation, are among some of the significant risk factors.*

HARLOW'S MONKEYS
Page 30
PAVLOV & CLASSICAL CONDITIONING
Page 32
PERCEPTIONS THAT DRIVE YOUR MOOD
Page 68

EATING DISORDERS: BEYOND FOOD

THE MAIN CONCEPT | On the surface, eating disorders may seem like a physical ailment. But they are serious, complex, and sometimes fatal mental health conditions, and they rank among the most common psychiatric problems faced by women in the Western world. Eating disorders lead to a host of issues, including depression, low self-esteem, sleep problems, anxiety, menstrual cessation, body dysmorphia—and premature death. The terms anorexia nervosa and bulimia nervosa are now familiar worldwide. Binge eating disorder is a third, and there are others, too, including compulsive night eating. Anorexia is characterized by an intense fear of being overweight, and continues even when someone's actual body weight is dangerously low. Bulimia, with its cycle of bingeing and purging, is marked by guilt about these episodes, often kept secret from friends or family. Binge eating involves the rapid consumption of large amounts of highly calorific foods in a short space of time and on a recurring basis, with a loss of control followed by extreme feelings of distress, disgust, and guilt. The causes of eating disorders are many (see opposite) and are both biological and social. Concern with body image is nothing new, but it seems to have heightened in our age of social media, where the idealization of thin, perfectly preened bodies is present everywhere.

THE BEAUTY BIAS
Page 112

SELIGMAN & DEPRESSION
Page 138

DRIVEN TO DISTRACTION
Page 144

THE EVIDENCE | In 2007, Ruth Striegel Weissman and Cynthia Bulik made a meta-analysis of dozens of existing studies of risk factors involved in developing an eating disorder. According to their findings, genetic factors, such as close relatives with an eating disorder, are a significant factor. So is the presence of an existing anxiety disorder, and certain personality traits, including perfectionism, social anxiety, and impulsivity, with the latter, predictably, exacerbating binge eating. There are also a multitude of environmental factors—notably the cultural obsession with the "thin beauty ideal" and the body dissatisfaction it can provoke. However, the single most common markers for developing an eating disorder are adolescence, and being female.

THE WIDER PICTURE | *Sufferers of eating disorders not only have to bear the social stigma attached to the illness, but plenty of myths and misconceptions, too. Contrary to popular belief, eating disorders are not a cry for attention and people can't just "get over it." Common treatments aim to tackle the anxieties and compulsions, often using temporary residential care with social support networks and talking therapy.*

SHUTTERED BY SCHIZOPHRENIA

THE MAIN CONCEPT | Schizophrenia—with its origins in the Greek words for "split" and "mind"—is one of the most serious types of psychiatric disorder. Symptoms include disorganized thoughts and distortions of reality (including hallucinations and delusions), along with a host of so-called "negative" symptoms that include social withdrawal, aimlessness, and "flattened" emotions, leading to severe difficulties with interpersonal relations. Genetic factors account for about 60 percent of the liability to develop schizophrenia, but studies of twins show that people with the genetic disposition do not necessarily go on to develop the illness, suggesting that social factors are at work, too. In fact a great deal of psychological research is now looking at how cognitive processes and coping skills can be developed to help patients deal with stressful events, reinforcing and complementing the medications that are designed to alter patients' brain functioning. As Ian Nicholson and Richard Neufeld observed in 1992, the two work together. Antipsychotic medication can help a patient retrieve ways of coping with life that were shut off by the illness, but cognitive and skills training—whether in groups or individually—can be needed to help the patient adapt existing skills to the everyday challenges of communal living, and, crucially, tackle those negative symptoms that medication has so far struggled to address.

THE EVIDENCE | Symptoms of schizophrenia like flattened emotions and social withdrawal have been the least responsive to antipsychotic medication, but they have been the subject of much research into non-medical therapeutic interventions. According to a detailed 2016 survey by André Aleman and colleagues, social skills training (SST) remains the most intensively studied, targeting communication skills to help social functioning; in 2014 David Turner and others had found that this was proving more effective than many other interventions. Cognitive Behavioral Therapy for psychosis (CBTp) has also been effective in reducing symptoms, while a newer therapy called Motivation and Enhancement Therapy (MOVE) is combining aspects of SST, CBTp, and other interventions in a bid to reach all of the various negative symptoms.

THE WIDER PICTURE | *Some clinicians (such as Jim van Os) would like to ditch the description of schizophrenia as an illness, and instead view its symptoms as part of a wider psychosis spectrum disorder—where discrete symptoms such as disorganized thinking, delusions, apathy, and numbed emotions can show up in a mild way in the general population, and most strongly in extreme cases.*

PERCEPTIONS THAT DRIVE YOUR MOOD
Page 68

ON BEING SANE IN INSANE PLACES
Page 134

NORMALITY: WHO'S THE JUDGE?
Page 136

DRIVEN TO DISTRACTION

THE MAIN CONCEPT | Anxiety is something that we can all feel from time to time. But if it is so intense that it, or our efforts to deal with it, get in the way of a normal life then it becomes an anxiety disorder. One fairly common example is the phobia, based on an irrational fear of something specific—something that is external to the individual affected, like a spider, or boarding a plane. However, there is another class of anxiety disorder—obsessive compulsive disorder (OCD), which is based on something that is going on inside our heads. The obsessive part relates to a fear or anxiety often linked to some kind of harm avoidance, such as fear of disease, or robbery, or contamination, or losing something valuable. The compulsive aspect is found in the ritualized behaviors to try to deal with this anxiety, such as constantly checking that the door is locked, the gas is off, hands are clean, or that nothing that may be needed in the future is ever thrown away. While the ritualized behavior is seen as providing relief to some OCD suffers, it can cause others to feel even more anxious, as examined in a paper by Gertina van Schalkwyk and others in 2016. What's more, ritualized checking (see opposite) appears to become self-defeating: the more often you check, the less you'll remember, necessitating yet more checking.

BARON-COHEN & AUTISM
Page 46

PERCEPTIONS THAT DRIVE YOUR MOOD
Page 68

EATING DISORDERS: BEYOND FOOD
Page 140

THE WIDER PICTURE | *Obsessive and compulsive behaviors are a feature of many illnesses, so the term OCD has been broadened to OCD spectrum disorders, grouping together a wide range of disorders in three main categories: compulsion disorders, including sexual compulsions and addictions to shopping or gambling; bodily preoccupations, including anorexia, bulimia, and body dysmorphia; and neurological disorders such as Tourette's syndrome and autism.*

THE EVIDENCE | In 2003, Marcel van den Hout and Merel Kindt explored why obsessive "checkers" (e.g., is the gas turned off?) have such low confidence in their memory of the last time they checked. They created a "virtual" gas stove, with mouse-activated control knobs for each of six "burners." Healthy participants were tasked with turning on and off varying combinations of burners 20 times, each time clicking back to check the burners were off. A second group operated the gas burners just once at the start, and once again at the end, performing an unrelated task in between. In a subsequent questionnaire, the group that repeatedly checked the gas showed a marked decrease in confidence in their memory at the end of the experiment: the more often we check, the less we trust what we have seen.

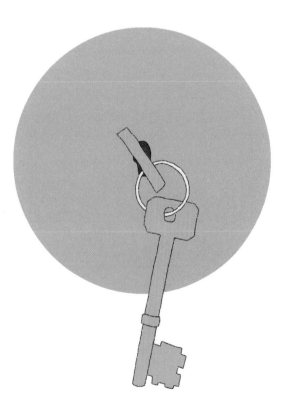

MIND SHARE

THE MAIN CONCEPT | "I can't believe this is happening to me!" When the going gets tough, we sometimes seek to "dissociate" ourselves from what's going on. An extreme—and rare—version of this reaction, usually in the face of very severe traumatic events, is known as dissociative identity disorder (DID), where the sufferer appears to take flight not only from events, but into a completely distinct personality—or personalities. Extreme cases of DID (formerly called multiple personality disorder) have involved radically different personalities, sometimes each with a separate set of memories and skills. A classic case was that of Chris Sizemore, a female patient who was treated by the psychiatrists Corbett Thigpen and Hervey Cleckley, and who provided the inspiration for the central character in the 1957 movie *The Three Faces of Eve*. Typically, patients maintain a dominant personality—the "host"—and secondary personalities known as "alters." The personality differences can be striking, involving marked differences in handwriting, memory, posture, ways of speaking, and personal histories, as well as perceptions of age, race, gender, or sexual orientation. There can also be significant amnesia, so one personality may be totally unaware of the experiences of another—opening the way to vast differences in learning, behavior, and ethics. The condition also throws up a host of legal issues, linked with responsibility in both criminal and civil law.

REPRESSION OF MEMORIES
Page 60

HOW FEELINGS BRING ON MEMORIES
Page 66

SHUTTERED BY SCHIZOPHRENIA
Page 142

THE EVIDENCE | As Thigpen and Cleckley noted in their fascinating paper on Chris Sizemore, multiple personality is like a myth—written about in history, but not "commonly encountered in the full reality of life." They put the record straight with their account of 14 months of therapy with the 25-year-old married woman, whom they were treating for headaches and blackouts. Soon after therapy began, the patient "Eve White," who was vulnerable, careworn, and anxious, came to therapy in her "alter" identity, as "Eve Black," who was confident and reckless, and looked and sounded very different. White knew nothing of Eve Black, but Black was aware of Eve White. The two identities had coexisted in the patient's mind, sharing the same past but becoming almost complete opposites in character. After eight months, a third personality, Jane, also appeared.

THE WIDER PICTURE | *Where does dissociative identity disorder come from? There are two main views. The "trauma theory" maintains that the causes lie in early and severe childhood physical or sexual trauma. In opposition to this is the "fantasy theory," which maintains that the patient plays a more conscious part in its creation. The two theories coexist in opposition to each other, not unlike the personalities of the sufferers themselves.*

GLOSSARY

ANXIETY—a feeling of unease, such as worry or fear, which can vary in severity.

ATTRIBUTION—assigning reasons for why things happen.

AUTISM—a lifelong developmental difficulty that affects how a person communicates and relates to other people, and how they experience the world around them.

BIG FIVE—in personality trait theory, also known as the Five-Factor Model. The five traits are Openness, Conscientiousness, Extraversion, Agreeableness, and Neuroticism.

BYSTANDER EFFECT—when the presence of other people during an emergency situation appears to prevent people from intervening to give assistance.

CLASSICAL CONDITIONING—a learning process observable in humans or animals, where two stimuli are linked together to produce a new behavior pattern. Pavlov's dogs provide the most famous example.

COGNITIVE BEHAVIORAL THERAPY—a form of psychotherapy based on cognitive psychology, which teaches people to modify dysfunctional thinking and behavior.

COGNITIVE DISSONANCE—a sense of unease caused by holding beliefs that disagree with each other.

CONFEDERATES—participants in a psychology experiment, secretly briefed to behave a certain way.

CONFIRMATION BIAS—a tendency to seek, believe, and retain information that confirms one's pre-existing beliefs.

CONTROL GROUP—in an experimental context, the participants who do not receive the experimental treatment for comparison purposes.

CORTISOL—a hormone released by the adrenal glands when a person experiences stress. Sometimes called the "stress hormone."

DEINDIVIDUATION—a reduction in self-awareness and self-control experienced in group situations.

DEPRESSION—a disorder marked by strong feelings of sadness and/or guilt; loss of motivation and energy; disturbances of sleep and diet; and an absence of any sense of pleasure.

DISSOCIATION—a sense of disconnect between a person and their feelings and thoughts, as well as with the world around them.

DISSOCIATIVE IDENTITY DISORDER—(formerly multiple personality disorder), DID is characterized by a person living with multiple separate and distinguishable personality states.

DSM— the American Psychiatric Association's *Diagnostic and Statistical Manual of Mental Disorders*.

ECOLOGICAL VALIDITY—the extent to which findings from a study or experiment can be generalized to the real world.

EGO—the part of the id that mediates with and is shaped by external reality (from Freud's "structural theory").

EPISODIC MEMORY—a person's memory of a specific event, at a specific time and place.

FACTOR ANALYSIS—a statistical method for studying the correlations between data to identify groups or clusters relying on a common factor.

FLASHBULB MEMORY—a vivid memory produced by an emotionally charged and often unexpected event.

FUNDAMENTAL ATTRIBUTION ERROR—a tendency to attribute other people's actions to personality traits, while attributing one's own actions to the situation at the time.

GESTALT PSYCHOLOGY—a strand of psychology that sees humans as striving for a wholeness of experience.

GROUPTHINK—a mode of thinking and decision-making that occurs when a group works closely together, often facing an external threat, and rejecting outside opinions or information.

HIERARCHY OF NEEDS—Abraham Maslow's theory proposing that humans have groups of needs to be roughly satisfied in sequence, ranging from basic needs (food and safety) up to self-fulfillment.

HUMANISTIC PSYCHOLOGY—a branch of psychology that focuses on achieving selfhood and one's full potential.

ID—the instinctive and unconscious part of the mind (within Freud's "structural theory").

INTROSPECTION—a process of self-reflection from which a person may observe their own perceptions, thoughts, feelings, or beliefs.

JAMES–LANGE THEORY OF EMOTION—the hypothesis that the experience of emotion is derived from bodily reactions, which are a response to some kind of external stimulus.

LEARNED HELPLESSNESS—a mechanism whereby being forced into a situation of helplessness in one unpleasant situation can lead to a sense of helplessness in other negative scenarios.

NEGATIVE SYMPTOMS—in the context of schizophrenia, these manifest as a loss of normal functioning, and include apathy, a lack of emotional feeling, and inhibited speech.

OBSESSIVE COMPULSIVE DISORDER—an anxiety disorder where a person has obtrusive distressing thoughts (obsessive thoughts) accompanied by compulsive behaviors.

OPERANT CONDITIONING—where learning is influenced by positive or negative outcomes, such as reward or punishment.

PHOBIA—an anxiety disorder characterized by an intense and irrational fear.

PLACEBO—a treatment or process that leads to an effect simply because the patient believes it is beneficial.

POSITIVE SYMPTOMS—a term for symptoms of schizophrenia, which include hallucinations, and delusions.

POST-TRAUMATIC STRESS DISORDER—a chronic disorder typically following a stressful experience, characterized by nightmares, flashbacks, and dissociation.

PSYCHOGENIC DISORDER—a disorder where the origins are psychological, rather than physical.

REPRESSION—from psychoanalytic theory, a defensive mechanism where thoughts are pushed into the unconscious.

SELF-ACTUALIZATION—in humanistic psychology models, achievement of one's full potential.

SENSORIMOTOR INTELLIGENCE—the learning and development stage of infants between birth and around two years of age.

SITUATIONISM—the idea that human personality is partly determined by the situation one is in, rather than solely by genetic factors.

SOCIAL COGNITIVE THEORY—a development of social learning theory, examining the interplay of a person, their experience, the environment, and the social setting in which learning and development takes place.

STEREOTYPE THREAT—when a stigma attached to a particular social group negatively affects the performance of a member of that group in a task where the stigma is perceived to be relevant.

STIMULUS-RESPONSE (SR)—behaviorist psychologists such as Ivan Pavlov, B. F. Skinner, and John B. Watson believed that all animal (including human) behavior could be attributed to innate or learned responses to external stimuli.

SUPER-EGO—the part of the mind that reflects society's norms and rules, learned from one's parents, contributing to conscience and guilt (within Freud's "structural theory").

TRAIT THEORY—an approach to personality psychology which holds that individual differences can be the result of innate traits that consistently predispose a person to act in a certain way.

UNCONSCIOUS—within Freud's "topographical theory" of the mind, the store of thoughts, urges, or memories— often unpleasant and repressed—and a major influence on human behavior.

FURTHER READING

Ainsworth, Mary, Mary Blehar, Everett Waters, and Sally Wall. *Patterns of Attachment: A Psychological Study of the Strange Situation*. New York: Psychology Press, 2015.

Aleman André, Tania Lincoln, Richard Bruggeman, Ingrid Melle, Johan Arends, Celso Arango, and Henderikus Knegtering. "Treatment of Negative Symptoms: Where Do We Stand, and Where Do We Go?" *Schizophrenia Research*, vol. 186 (2017): 55–62.

Allen, Andrea, Audrey King, and Eric Hollander. "Obsessive-Compulsive Spectrum Disorders." *Dialogues in Clinical Neuroscience*, vol. 5, no. 3 (2003): 259–71.

Asch, Solomon. *Social Psychology*. Englewood Cliffs, NJ: Prentice-Hall, 1952.

Bandura, Albert, Dorothea Ross, and Sheila Ross. "Transmission of Aggression through Imitation of Aggressive Models." *Journal of Abnormal and Social Psychology*, vol. 63, no. 3 (1961): 575–82.

Baron-Cohen, Simon. *Autism and Asperger Syndrome (The Facts)*. Oxford: OUP, 2008.

Baumeister, Roy, Ellen Bratslavsky, Mark Muraven, and Dianne Tice. "Ego Depletion: Is the Active Self a Limited Resource?" *Journal of Personality and Social Psychology*, vol. 74, no. 5 (1998) 1252–65.

Beck, Aaron T. *Depression: Causes and Treatment*. Philadelphia: University of Philadelphia Press, 1967.

Bowlby, John. *A Secure Base: Parent-Child Attachment and Healthy Human Development*. London: Routledge, 1988.

Butler, Judith. *Gender Trouble: Feminism and the Subversion of Identity*. New York: Routledge, 2006.

Damasio, Antonio. *Descartes' Error: Emotion, Reason, and the Human Brain*. New York: G. P. Putnam, 1994.

Diener, Ed. "Deindividuation, Self-Awareness, and Disinhibition." *Journal of Personality and Social Psychology*, vol. 37, no. 7 (1979): 1160–71.

Dion, Karen, Ellen Berscheid, and Elaine Walster. "What Is Beautiful Is Good." *Journal of Personality and Social Psychology*, vol. 24, no. 3 (1972): 285–90.

Duckworth, Angela. *Grit: The Power of Passion and Perseverance*. New York: Scribner, 2016.

Dweck, Caroline, and Elaine Elliot. "Goals: An approach to Motivation and Achievement." *Journal of Personality and Social Psychology*, vol. 54, no. 1 (1988): 5–12.

Ericsson, Anders, Ralf Krampe, and Clemens Tesch-Romer. "The Role of

Deliberate Practice in the Acquisition of Expert Performance." *Psychological Review*, vol. 100, no. 3 (1993): 363–406.

Erinosho, Olayiwola, and Akolawole Ayonrinde (1981). "A Comparative Study of Opinion and Knowledge about Mental Illness in Different Societies." *Psychiatry*, vol. 41, no. 4 (1978): 403–10.

Eysenck, Hans. *Dimensions of Personality*. Oxford: Kegan Paul, 1947.

Freud, Sigmund (1915). "Repression." In *Sigmund Freud. Collected Papers*, vol. IV, Chapter V. London: Hogarth Press.

Funk, Cary, and Brian Kennedy. *The Politics of Climate*. PEW Research Center, 2016.

Harlow, Harry. "Love in Infant Monkeys." *Scientific American*, vol. 200 (1959): 68–74.

Kohlberg, Lawrence. *Stages in the Development of Moral Thought and Action*. New York: Holt Rinehart & Winston, 1969.

Langlois, Judith, and Cookie Stephan. "The Effects of Physical Attractiveness and Ethnicity on Children's Behavioral Attributions and Peer Preferences." *Child Development*, vol. 48 (1977): 1694.

Latané, Bibb, and John Darley, "Bystander 'Apathy'." *American Scientist*, vol. 57 (1969): 244–68.

Latané, Bibb, Kipling Williams, and Stephen Harkins. "Many Hands Make Light the Work: The Causes and Consequences of Social Loafing." *Journal of Personality and Social Psychology*, vol. 37, no. 6 (1979): 822–32.

Loftus, Elizabeth. *Eyewitness Testimony*. Cambridge, MA: Harvard University Press, 1979.

Loftus, Elizabeth, and John Palmer. "Reconstruction of Automobile Destruction: An Example of the Interaction between Language and Memory." *Journal of Verbal Learning and Behavior*, vol. 13 (1974): 585–89.

Lowry, Richard. *A. H. Maslow: An Intellectual Portrait*. Pacific Grove, CA: Brooks/Cole, 1973.

Macmillan, Malcolm. "Phineas Gage: Unravelling the Myth." *The Psychologist*, vol. 21, no 9 (2008).

Maier, Steven, and Martin Seligman, "Learned Helplessness: Theory and Evidence." *Journal of Experimental Psychology: General*, vol. 105, no. 1 (1976): 3–46.

Maslow, Abraham. "A Theory of Human Motivation." *Psychological Review*, vol. 50, no. 4 (1943): 370–96.

Milgram, Stanley. *Obedience to Authority*. New York: Harper & Row, 1974.

Miller, George A. "The Magical Number Seven, Plus or Minus Two: Some Limitations on Our Capacity for Processing Information." *Psychological Review*, vol. 63 (1956): 81–97.

Mischel, Walter. *The Marshmallow Test: Mastering Self-Control*. New York: Little, Brown, 2014.

Moscovici, Serge, Elisabeth Lage, and Martine Naffrechoux. "Influence of a Consistent Minority on the Responses of a Majority in a Color Perception Task." *Sociometry*, vol. 32 (1969): 365–80.

Munro, Geoffrey. "The Scientific Impotence Excuse: Discounting Belief-Threatening Scientific Abstracts," *Journal of Applied Social Psychology*, vol. 40, no. 3 (2010): 579–600.

Pavlov, Ivan. *Conditioned Reflexes*, Oxford: OUP, 1927.

Piaget, Jean. *The Origin of Intelligence in Children*. New York: International Universities Press, 1952.

Rogers, Carl. *On Becoming a Person: A Therapist's View of Psychotherapy*. Boston: Houghton Mifflin Company, 1961.

Rosenhan, David. "On Being Sane in Insane Places." *Science*, vol. 179 (1973): 250–57.

Rushton, Philippe, and Roland Chrisjohn. "Extraversion, Neuroticism, Psychoticism and Self-Reported Delinquency: Evidence from Eight Separate Samples." *Personality and Individual Differences*, vol. 2, no. 1 (1981): 11–20.

Rutter, Michael. *Maternal Deprivation Reassessed* (2nd edition). Harmondsworth: Penguin, 1981.

Sachs, Jacqueline, Barbara Bard, and Marie Johnson. "Language Learning with Restricted Input: Case Studies of Two Hearing Children of Deaf Parents." *Applied Psycholinguistics*, vol. 2, no. 1 (1981): 33–54.

Schachter, Stanley, and Jerome Singer. "Cognitive, Social, and Physiological Determinants of Emotional State." *Psychological Review*, vol. 69 (1962): 379–99.

Shoda, Yuichi, Walter Mischel, and Jack Wright. "Intraindividual Stability in the Organization and Patterning of Behavior." *Journal of Personality and Social Psychology*, vol. 67, no. 4 (1994): 674–87.

Siegel, Jane, Vitaly Dubrovsky, Sara Kiesler, and Timothy McGuire. "Group Processes in Computer-Mediated Communication." *Organizational Behavior and Human Decision Processes*, vol. 37, no. 2 (1986): 157–87.

Smetana, Judith. "Preschool Children's Conceptions of Moral and Social Rules." *Child Development*, vol. 52 (1981): 1333–36.

Smith, Caroline, and Barbara Lloyd. "Maternal Behavior and Perceived Sex of Infant: Revisited." *Child Development*, vol. 49, no. 4 (1978): 1263–65.

Steele, Claude. *Whistling Vivaldi and Other Clues to How Stereotypes Affect Us*. New York: WW Norton, 2010.

Steele, Claude, and Joshua Aronson. "Stereotype Threat and the Intellectual Test Performance of African-Americans." *Journal of Personality and Social Psychology*, vol. 69, no. 5 (1995): 797–811.

Tajfel, Henri. "Experiments in Intergroup Discrimination." *Scientific American*, vol. 223 (1973): 96–102.

Thigpen, Corbett, and Hervey Cleckley. "A Case of Multiple Personality." *The Journal of Abnormal and Social Psychology*, vol. 49, no. 1 (1954): 135–51.

Thomas, Kyle, Julian De Freitas, Peter DeScioli, and Steven Pinker. "Recursive Mentalizing and Common Knowledge in the Bystander Effect." *Journal of Experimental Psychology: General*, vol. 145, no. 5 (2016): 621–29.

Turkheimer, Eric, Andreana Haley, Mary Waldron, Brian D'Onofrio, and Irving Gottesman. "Socioeconomic Status Modifies Heritability of IQ in Young Children." *Psychological Science*, vol. 14, no. 6 (2003).

van den Hout, Marcel, and Merel Kindt. "Obsessive-Compulsive Disorder and the Paradoxical Effects of Perseverative Behavior on Experienced Uncertainty." *Journal of Behavior Therapy and Experimental Psychiatry*, vol. 35 (2004): 165–81.

Vermeir, Iris, and Dieneke Van de Sompel. "Assessing the What Is Beautiful Is Good Stereotype." *Journal of Consumer Policy*, vol. 37 (2013).

Vygotsky, Lev. *Thought and Language*. Cambridge, MA: MIT Press, 1962.

Weissman, Ruth, and Cynthia, Bulik. "Risk Factors for Eating Disorders." *The American Psychologist*, vol. 62 (2007): 181–98.

Williams, Kipling, Steve Nida, Lawrence Baca, and Bibb Latané. "Social Loafing and Swimming." *Basic and Applied Social Psychology*, vol. 10, no. 1 (1989): 73–81.

Zimbardo, Philip. *The Lucifer Effect: Understanding How Good People Turn Evil*. New York: Random House, 2007. See also www.prisonexp.org.

INDEX

36 Questions That Lead to Love, The 87, 114–15

A
abnormality, criteria for 119, 136–37
Abramson, Lyn 68
Abu Ghraib 97
achievement motivation 50–51
Ainsworth, Mary 22, 25, 26–27
Aleman, André 143
Allport, Floyd 120, 124
Allport, Gordon 89, 118, 120
Altman, Irwin 114
anorexia nervosa 140–41
Aron, Arthur 87, 114–15
Aronson, Joshua 103
Asch, Solomon 86, 88, 90–91
attachment theory 22, 26–27
autism 46–47, 148
Ax, Albert 72
Ayonrinde, Akolawole 137

B
Baddeley, Alan 59
Bandura, Albert 23, 25, 40–41, 50, 128
Bard, Barbara 45
Baron-Cohen, Simon 23, 46–47
Bartlett, Frederic 54, 62
Baumeister, Roy 55, 76–77
Bay of Pigs invasion 101
beauty bias 112–13, 141
Beck, Aaron T. 15, 19, 55, 57, 68–69, 138
behavioral psychology 12–13
Berscheid, Ellen 112, 113
Big Five model 118, 126–27, 148
Binet, Alfred 130
binge eating 140–41
Bobo doll experiment 25, 40–41

Bosnian war crimes 97
Bower, Gordon 66–67
Bowlby, John 20, 22, 24, 28–29
Broca, Paul 122
Brown, George 139
Bruner, Jerome 56
Bulik, Cynthia 141
bulimia 140–41
Burt, Cyril 120
Butler, Judith 49
bystander effect 87, 98–99, 148

C
Cannon, Walter 72
Carlsmith, James 65
Cattell, Raymond 118, 120, 124
Chameleon Man 127
Chomsky, Noam 14, 23, 44–45
Chrisjohn, Roland 125
Clark, James 61
classical conditioning 12–13, 32–33, 148
Cleckley, Hervey 146, 147
Cognitive Affective Personality System (CAPS) 121
Cognitive Behavioral Therapy 15, 68–69, 148
cognitive development 34–37
cognitive dissonance 54, 64–65, 88, 148
cognitive psychology 14–15
collective unconscious 10
Comer, Ronald 136
conditioning
    classical 12–13, 32–33
    operant 13
confirmation bias 54, 82–83
conformity, need for 49, 90–91
Conway, Martin 62
Costa, Paul 126
Csikszentmihalyi, Mihaly 80–81

D
Damasio, Antonio 74–75
D'Andrade, Roy 50
Darley, John 98–99
Darwin, Charles 70
decision-making 74–75
deindividuation 87, 111, 148
depression 15, 138–39
    and cognitive therapy 68–69
    diagnoses of mental illness 134–37
Diener, Ed 110
Dion, Karen 112, 113
dissociative identity disorder 146–47
DSM (Diagnostic and Statistical Manual of Mental Disorders) 19, 134, 148
Duckworth, Angela 50
Dweck, Carol 23, 50, 51

E
eating disorders 140–41
Ebbinghaus, Hermann 12, 18, 54
ego 10, 118, 148
"ego depletion" 76–77
eight stages of man 38–39
Ekman, Paul 70–71
Elliot, Elaine 51
Ellis, Albert 15
emojis 70–71
emotions
    and decision-making 74–75
    and memory 66–67
    theories of 72–73
    universality of 70–71
EPQ test (the Eysenck Personality Questionnaire) 118, 124–25
Ericsson, Anders 119, 132, 133
Erikson, Erik 23, 38–39

Erinosho, Olayiwola 137
Eysenck, Hans Jürgen 118,
  121, 124–25

F
"factor analysis" 118, 118,
  120, 149
fake news 82–83
false memories 57, 61, 62–63
Ference, Richard 100
Ferrier, David 122
Festinger, Leon 64–65
flashbulb memories 62, 149
flow 80–81
Freud, Anna 11
Freud, Sigmund 6, 10–11, 18,
  22, 40, 56, 60, 118
Friesen, Walter 71
fundamental attribution error
  55, 78–79, 149

G
Gage, Phineas 123
Galen 122
Galton, Francis 132
gender identity 48–49
genius 132–3
Genovese, Catherine "Kitty" 98
Gestalt psychology 88, 149
"groupthink" 86, 100–101,
  149
Guntrip, Harry 11

H
Hagger, Martin 76
Hambrick, David 132
Harkins, Stephen 108–109
Harlow, Harry 22, 30–31
Harlow, Dr. John 123
Harris, Tirril 139
Harvard Center for Cognitive
  Studies 14, 19, 56
hierarchy of needs 16, 17, 87,
  106–107, 149
Hitch, Graham 59

Holocaust 94, 97
Hout, Marcel van den 145
humanistic psychology 16–17
humors 122

I
id 10, 118, 150
intelligence
  genius 132–33
  IQ tests 130–31

J
Jack, Rachael 70
James, William 12, 18, 58, 72
James–Lange theory of
  emotion 72, 149
Janis, Irving 86, 100–101
Johns Hopkins University 18
Johnson, Marie 45
Jung, Carl 10, 18

K
Kahneman, Daniel 19
Karau, Steven 109
Kennedy, John F. 101
Kenrick, Douglas 107
Kindt, Merel 145
Klein, Melanie 11
Klein, Paul 61
Kohlberg, Lawrence 23, 42–43
Köhler, Wolfgang 88
Kraepelin, Emil 134
Krampe, Ralf 133
Krems, Jaimie 107

L
Lange, Carl 72
Langlois, Judith 112
language, development 44–45
Latané, Bibb 98–99, 108–109
Le Bon, Gustave 110
learned helplessness 139, 149
Levina, Rosa 37
Levinger, George 61
Little Albert 13

Lloyd, Barbara 49
Loftus, Elizabeth 52, 54, 57,
  62–63
love, research into 114

M
McCrae, Robert 126
magic number 58–59
Maier, Steven 139
Martz, Denise 112
Maslow, Abraham 16, 80, 87,
  106–107
maternal deprivation theory
  28–29
memory
  and emotion 66–67
  false memories 57, 61,
    62–63
  "magic number" 58–59
  repression of memories
    60–61
Milgram, Stanley 19, 86, 89,
  94–95
Miller, George A. 54, 56,
  58–59
minority influence theory
  92–93
Mischel, Walter 116, 118, 121,
  126–27, 129
mob mentality 87
mob psychology 110–11
Moorhead, Gregory 100
morality 42–43
Moscovici, Serge 86, 92–93
Moseley, Winston 98
multiple personality disorder
  see dissociative identity
  disorder
Munro, Geoffrey 83

N
Neck, Chris 100
Neel, Rebecca 107
Neisser, Ulric 14, 62
Nemeth, Charlan 93

Neufeld, Richard 142
Nicholson, Ian 142
Nisbett, Richard 79
Norman, Warren 126

O
Obama, Barack 76
obedience experiments 19,
  86, 94–95
object relations, school of 11
obsessive compulsive
  disorder (OCD) 144–45, 150
Odbert, Henry 124
Oedipus Complex 10, 22
operant conditioning 13, 149
Os, Jim van 143
Osgood, Charles 70

P
Palmer, John 63
Pavlov, Ivan 12, 23, 32–3
person-centered therapy
  16–17
personality
  early theories 122–23
  questionnaires 124–25
  social cognitive theory
    128–29
  trait theory 121, 126–27
phrenology 118, 122
Piaget, Jean 14, 18, 23, 24,
  34–35, 36, 42
Pollack, Irwin 59
positive psychology 17
psychoanalysis 10–11, 118

Q
Q Sort test 17
questionnaires 124–25

R
repression of memories
  60–61
Riecken, Henry 64
Ringelmann, Max 108

Robber's Cave experiment 96
Rogers, Carl 16–17, 107
Rosen, Bernard 50
Rosenhan, David 119, 134–35,
  136
Ross, Dorothea 41
Ross, Lee 55, 78–79
Ross, Sheila 41
Rushton, Philippe 125
Russia, Stalinist 97
Rutter, Michael 29

S
Sachs, Jacqueline 45
Schachter, Stanley 64, 72–73
Schalkwyk, Gertina van 144
schizophrenia 142–43
Schoda, Yuichi 127
self-actualization 80,
  106–107, 151
self-concept 17
Seligman, Martin 68, 119,
  136, 138, 139
Sherif, Muzafer and Carolyn
  96
Shoda, Yuichi 121
Siegel, Jane 111
Simon, Theodore 24, 130
Singer, Jerome 72–73
Sizemore, Chris 146, 147
Skinner, B. F. 13, 40, 44
Skinner's Box 13
Sloan, Dick 109
Smetana, Judith 43
Smith, Caroline 49
Snyder, Mark 127
social cognitive theory
  128–29, 151
social identity theory 87,
  104–105
social learning theory 40–41,
  128
social loafing 87, 108–9
Stanford "Prison" Experiment
  19, 86, 96–97

Steele, Claude 86, 88,
  102–103
Stephan, Cookie 112
stereotype threat 86, 88,
  102–103
stimulus-response (SR)
  12–13, 151
Stone, Jeff 102
super-ego 10, 118, 151

T
Tajfel, Henri 86–87, 89,
  104–105
Taylor, Dalmas 114
Teasdale, John 68
Tesch-Romer, Clemens 133
Thigpen, Corbett 146, 147
The 36 Questions That Lead
  to Love, 87, 114–15
Thomas, Kyle 99
timeline 18–19
trait theory 121, 126–27, 151
Turkheimer, Eric 130, 131
Turner, David 143

V
Vaillant, George 39
Van de Sompel, Dieneke 113
Vermeir, Iris 113
Vygotsky, Lev 14, 23, 36–37

W
Walster, Elaine 112, 113
Watson, John B. 12–13, 18, 30,
  40, 132
Weissman, Ruth Striegel 141
Wertheimer, Max 88
Williams, Kipling 108–109
Winnicott, Donald 11
Wright, Jack 127
Wundt, Wilhelm 12, 18

Z
Zimbardo, Philip 84, 86, 95,
  96–97, 110

ABOUT THE AUTHORS

Paul Carslake is a writer, journalist, and translator, and has been a publisher of non-fiction books for more than a decade, spending much of his career trying to tease complex subjects into accessible and appealing formats that can engage any reader. He has a degree in Philosophy, Politics, and Economics from the University of Oxford, and is currently completing an MSc in Psychodynamic Counselling and Psychotherapy at London University's Birkbeck College. He lives in London, England with his wife, daughter, and two cats.

Razwana Quadir is a Communications Manager based at the University of Southampton, England. With a BA Hons/MA in Politics, Psychology and Sociology, and Management Studies from the University of Cambridge and the Cambridge Judge Business School, she is fascinated by how humans think, behave, and live in society. Razwana's interest in consumer psychology led her to work in marketing and communications since 2013 in both the private and public sector, alongside writing in her spare time and tutoring students in Psychology to degree level. She is interested in pursuing a future in psychotherapy and counseling.

ACKNOWLEDGMENTS

Paul Carslake Thanks to my co-author, Razwana, and to our editors Stephanie Evans, Angela Koo, Claire Saunders, and all at Ivy Press, and to our illustrator Elise Gaignet; thank you also to the great Nicky Hayes, author of *Foundations of Psychology*, a battered copy of which first got me thinking about this subject some years ago. Isabelle and Francesca, I'm indebted for your support and distractions respectively.

Razwana Quadir To all my teachers, especially those who inspired my love of psychology at Peter Symonds College; my supervisors at the University of Cambridge who deepened my knowledge further; my family for always supporting my education, and to all my friends, who are my biggest cheerleaders in all that I do. To everyone at Ivy Press who worked on this and for being so patient with it all. Thank you! And finally, Paul, thank you for your ongoing support and for offering me the wonderful opportunity to be a part of producing this book in the first place.

Picture credits

The publisher would like to thank the following individuals and organizations for permission to reproduce copyright material:

Getty Images /Bettman 18 (top right), 24 (bottom left), 120 (bottom left); /JHU Sheridan Libraries/Gado 25 (bottom left); / ullstein bild (Jan Rieckhoff) 24 (top right), 88 (bottom left), 89 top right; /Universal Images Group 18 (bottom left), 56 (bottom left)

George A. Miller 56 (top right), photograph © JT Miller, 2012

Shutterstock/Rex/ITV/Ken McKay 121 (top right)

Henri Tajfel 89 (bottom left), photograph courtesy of Peter Robinson. With grateful thanks to Rupert Brown for checking the text.

Raymond B. Cattell, 120 (top right) courtesy of University of Illinois, Portrait of Raymond B. Cattell, 1967. Found in RS 39/1/11, Box 14, Cattell, Raymond

Wikimedia Commons 25 (left); /BDEngler 57 (top left); /Sirswindon Photograph by Sybil Eysenck 121 (bottom right); /Slicata 57 (bottom left); /TeachAIDS, Stanford, CA 88 (top right)

All reasonable efforts have been made to trace copyright holders and to obtain their permission for the use of copyright material. The publisher apologizes for any errors or omissions in the list above and will gratefully incorporate any corrections in future reprints if notified.